NO LONGER
PROPERTY OF PPLD

D0047453

Bats, Rats, & Holy Cows
Or Seventeen Days in India

One family's adventure

NO LONGER
PROPERTY OF PPLD

NO LONGER
PROPERTY OF PPLD

Mariann Margulis

Copyright © 2012 Mariann Margulis
All rights reserved.

ISBN: 1468168398
ISBN 13: 9781468168396

Library of Congress Control Number: 2012900165
CreateSpace, North Charleston, SC

*This book is dedicated to my sons, Julian and Fillip,
who inspire me to travel, and my husband Tony,
who inspires me to write.*

Contents

Foreword

It hit me like a ton of bricks: curry—the smell of curry. It was definitely the smell of curry, mixed with some cardamom, chili, cumin, and nutmeg. It was all around me, getting into my nostrils, under my clothes, and into my hair. The smell was pungent and powerful; it was the kind of smell that irritated my throat and made my eyes water.

We were at the Continental Airlines terminal in New York boarding the flight to New Delhi. All around us were people who looked like they were going home or to their parents' homes, or perhaps to their in-laws'. Most of them were carrying huge bags. Judging by the smell emanating from these bags, these people were either transporting *dal* or all the ingredients to allow them to start making *dal* the minute they set foot on the plane. A young man next to us, sporting almost platinum blond hair that looked alarmingly bizarre next to his dark olive skin, was having a lengthy conversation with someone I hoped was paying for this call, all the while gesticulating wildly and nodding feverishly in between loud outbursts in a language I did not understand. A little old woman in a sari and a huge dangling nose ring adorned with a sparkling ruby was wheeled next to us to await boarding. For the last twenty minutes, she had been berating her son while wagging a long bony finger in front of his face. He looked totally uninterested and kept leafing through the pages of an Indian magazine while occasionally nodding at the old woman to show that he was, indeed, sincerely concerned.

What were we doing here? A sole non-Hindu woman with two adolescent sons, ages ten and twelve. Were we really going to get on that flight?

I had always wanted to visit India. Ever since I was a little kid, images of the Taj Mahal and elephants adorned in rich fabrics and dazzling jewels mesmerized me. As a child growing up in the Soviet Union, Bollywood movies were my only link to the world outside Russia and its puppet republics. Just like the country that produced them, these films were never average or serene. These were over-the-top productions where humor was mostly physical and tears were almost always due to a cheating spouse/boyfriend/girlfriend. All the women were beautiful and men gallant. And the ones who were not? Well, they played the servants who merged successfully with the colorful background.

And then there were the documentaries—hours and hours of stories about the ancient Aryan civilizations, followed by the glorious conquests of the Mughals and the riches of the jewel of the British Empire, and culminating with the Indian independence movement led by Mahatma Gandhi. But none of it enthralled me the way Benares did. I could watch program after program about cremation ghats, the holy river, and the ancient bathing rituals. Everything about Benares seemed primordial and holy. In a child's memory, Benares remained a magical place in a faraway land.

A few decades later, I had two kids of my own: Julian, twelve, and Fillip, ten. This was the third year the kids and I had been traveling by ourselves. My husband had launched a new business three years before and has been unable to take a vacation ever since, so it's been the three of us. Every vacation was jointly chosen by all three of us; we picked a place, agreed on an itinerary, and chose hotels by a majority vote. It all usually started in a bookstore. Sometime in February, the three of us would park ourselves in the coffee shop of a bookstore and proceed to go through the store's travel section. We would start at breakfast. No destination was off-limits; every continent was considered; and every country was examined. Thus, some time before dinner, by process of elimination, we would agree on our next vacation destination. This year was not any different. We sipped our lattes and green tea FRAPPUCINOS®, and the kids happily leafed through the pages of numerous travel guides. And then I saw it, somewhere between tomes on Ecuador and New Guinea: India.

"Hey, kids, what do you think of that?" I said, pointing at the book.

"It does look nice." OK, so far, so good.

"But we did consider Italy—"

"And Turkey—"

"How about China?"

I was so close.

By the fourth FRAPPUCINO, not only had the kids agreed to go to India, they insisted on it.

That was that. We were going to India. Next came a few hectic months of preparation. I knew nothing about India except the Taj Mahal and Benares (and even the latter was renamed Varanasi by that time). But weeks of research resulted in an itinerary that included trains, planes, and automobiles, with some rickshaws and camels thrown in. Then we had to consider the East Asia monsoons that hit the continent by late June and continue through the rest of the summer months. This pushed the trip up to the kids' spring break.

Then there was the matter of immunizations. Suddenly, diseases that I only had read about in history books needed to be vaccinated against—typhoid, diphtheria, dysentery, to say nothing of the malaria pills that only came in size extra large with a very convenient kids' dosage of three-quarters of a pill. Have you ever tried cutting a pill into three quarters? I strongly recommend it as a party game: cutting the pill. The object of the game is to save the pill and all your fingers. Finally, after weeks of research and e-mail exchanges with fellow travelers, it was decided that I would not attempt to drive a car in India. We were going to hire a driver.

A few months passed, and finally it was time for our trip. Little did we know that when we stepped onto that flight to New Delhi and flew halfway across the planet, we would be stepping into a different world and a different century.

Chapter 1

DEPARTURE

There were a few times, while we were waiting to board the plane, when I thought someone from the terminal would come over and escort us out. We just did not belong. With the exception of a few Hindu-looking businessmen who looked like they were being dragged back to the motherland, we were the only people who did not speak Hindi or carry *dal* ingredients in our bags. Heads turned the second we set foot in that terminal. What started out as few curious glances quickly escalated into an unabashed collective stare that continued until boarding. We were an oddity, and people did not hesitate to show us that. Little did we know that this shameless gawking would haunt us for the next two and a half weeks.

There is a small advantage to traveling with children: the chance to board the plane first. Needless to say, as soon as we heard that, off we went (preceded only by the sari-clad old woman who was still grumbling at her son). We happily put our bags into the overhead compartment and settled into our section of three seats when Julian noticed that our in-flight entertainment systems were off—all three of them. Being a good mother, I scolded him for caring about all the wrong things at the wrong time. I was still fussing with my bags and documents when Fillip decided to join his brother in complaining that the video systems were off. After reprimanding Fillip (I am, after all, an equal opportunity lecturer), I finally gave in and called the flight attendant.

I knew it would not be pretty when I saw the face on the male flight attendant approaching our row. As soon as he saw that a kid had pressed the call button, he became visibly annoyed, and it was clear from his expression that he was offended by our very presence.

"What is it, Ma'am?" I hate being called "Ma'am." I would rather be called anything else. This was going to be a long flight.

"Can you please take a look at our entertainment systems? While all others seem to be functioning, ours do not even power on."

"Ma'am, I have other passengers to greet and settle. I assure you there is nothing wrong with the system. It will be functioning once we are airborne." That did not sound credible, but I had a strong feeling that if I pressed him on it, he would just throw himself on the floor and start rolling around in hysterical convulsions. I was not going to be the cause of that. So I calmly explained to my children that the flight attendant knew his business and that they would have to be patient and wait until we were in the air.

An hour later, I was feverishly pressing the flight attendant call button myself. According to the pilot, our flight was going to be delayed on the runway for about two hours. As soon as the passengers heard that, they started flipping channels or pushing buttons on their entertainment centers to busy themselves before dinner. I tried to convince the kids to do some reading. After all, we were facing a fourteen-hour flight and were due to arrive in New Delhi at about seven o'clock at night. That was perfect for our jetlag, as we could just go to sleep upon our arrival at the hotel. Therefore, we did not need to sleep on the flight; we would busy ourselves with the books, and eventually, the movies and games available to each passenger on his or her entertainment center. I happily took out my book to forge ahead with the plan in my head when, to my horror, I realized that the overhead light, just like the entertainment centers, did not work. I imagined the next sixteen hours with no book, no movie, no games. – NOTHING!

"Yes, Ma'am, what is it now?" For a split second I imagined our flight attendant jumping on top of me and beating me unconscious.

"Can you please take a look at our row? It seems that not only the entertainment centers, but all of the electricity is out. I doubt that has to do with being airborne, right? Especially considering everyone else's is functioning just fine."

"I will see what I can do," hissed our flight martyr, and he disappeared behind the food concession curtain. He reappeared about ten minutes later with a woman he introduced as a flight supervisor. She proceeded to press every button on the entertainment system and the overhead panel. After about five minutes of this exercise, she declared that there was indeed something wrong with our section's power supply. About three hours and four power resets later, she happily informed me that she would not charge me for a glass of wine with my dinner, due to my troubles. At that moment, I would've happily bought her a bottle of a 2005 Reserve to just have power in at least one of our seats. Alas, it was not to be; because the flight was booked solid, we could not move. The kids spent most of the sixteen hours migrating between a few scattered single empty seats trying to occupy themselves with some games. I, on the other hand, spent that night looking for my kids (as a force of habit, I had the need to know where they were at all times) and observing the medical soap opera that unfolded on the flight about four hours after takeoff.

It started with an announcement of a sick passenger on board and a plea for a doctor. What ensued was a mass exodus of various specialists from first class, followed by a full medical consortium around the sari-clad old lady, who apparently had fallen ill (she was probably just exhausted from all that finger-wagging). All through the night, these various experts kept coming and going; some took the patient's pulse, others listened to her heart, and still others just debated something (hopefully her diagnosis, and not the latest Pakistani/Indian cricket match) with other experts—loudly in Hindi. Needless to say, there was no sleeping for anyone on that flight other than the sick patient. When she did not snore loudly between doctor visits, she loudly moaned about something to her son, the doctors, flight attendants, and generally anyone who was unfortunate enough to pass by her seat on the way to the lavatory. After numerous futile attempts at either entertainment or sleep, the kids and I settled in our seats for the last fun-filled four hours of the flight counting the "stans" over which we were passing—Kazakhstan, Afghanistan, Pakistan, and so on.

Chapter 2

ARRIVAL

"This is Mariann." My phone had begun to ring the minute I turned it on while trying to find the proper customs queue at the Indira Gandhi Airport in New Delhi. I could not believe it. I thought I had told all my clients I would be away. What was this one doing bothering me all the way from Parsippany? And why was I even answering it? I was feverishly trying to maneuver the phone in my hands while waving my other hands around my face, arms, and body, swatting away what seemed like an army of industrial-sized mosquitoes.

"You're not bothering me at all. No problem. How could you possibly remember that I'm away? No really, if it's not too much bother for you, call me back when I return."

Next to me, the kids were performing the same mosquito dance while our fellow passengers just stared at us with disdain and petulance. We spent the next thirty minutes on the customs queue violently jumping around, flailing our arms and slapping ourselves silly. All the while, our fellow passengers were merrily conducting conversations on their cell phones, which did not prevent them from keeping their disapproving glances fixed directly on the spectacle that was my family.

After a number of usual relevant questions from security (Are you carrying concealed weapons? Are you transporting potentially infectious food items?), we were finally out of the terminal and facing a sea of impatient relatives and friends meeting our flight. I was anxiously looking through the crowd in hopes of spotting our driver. I did not know his name or what he would look like. But the last e-mail I had received from the tour company assured me that he would be waiting for us at the airport. I kept walking right past a mustached man holding a sign that said "Mr. Magolez." And why not? It was not until he called out "Madame, Madame" that it occurred to me he was there to meet us. I suppose seeing a lone redhead with two pre-teens tipped him off. (Either that or there was something about my bulging eyes and pulsating neck vein that betrayed me as a New Yorker.)

"I am Kamal, and I am very pleased," said Kamal, and he placed a flower garland around my neck.

"You have no idea how pleased I am, Kamal," I replied, meaning every word. "I am Mariann, and these are my kids, Julian and Fillip."

"Very nice, Madame." I quickly realized that my name would be Madame for the next two weeks. Madame is Hindi for Mariann.

We walked to what looked like a rather comfortable Land Cruiser waiting for us in a parking lot. Never in a million years would I have pegged that dirt field with some randomly discarded cars as being a parking lot. But Kamal knew better. We were not even out of the airport grounds when I realized that I had done the right thing by hiring a driver. While Kamal skillfully maneuvered his Land Cruiser in and out of crowds of smoking teenagers, mothers with babies hanging from pouches on their backs, and wandering cows, I kept imagining myself circling around this live obstacle course and eventually breaking down in hysterics somewhere between the Air India and Air France terminals.

The air was hot and humid although it was after ten o'clock at night. Even with the car windows closed to allow for air-conditioning, we could feel the thickness and clamminess of the pre-monsoon New Delhi air. It was oppressive but not nearly as oppressive as the smells that hit our nostrils the second we set foot outside the terminal. Not that the terminal smelled like roses, but there was still an air (pardon the pun) of pretense around all those foreign flights that took off and landed at that huge international airport hub. Outside of it, however, New Delhi came alive; it was pulsating with honest, everyday life, full of sights, sounds, and smells that did not, or would not, allow for any interference from something so irrelevant and meaningless as the outside world.

Inside the Land Cruiser, the kids and I were glued to the car windows. The car's sleek outside turned out to be a facade for its old pleather-clad interior. It sported a long, narrow stick shift that rose from the floor between the two front seats. Every time Kamal's hand shifted gears, the stick bent like a dandelion in the wind, revealing itself to be way too thin for his heavy hands and dangerously fragile. In the back, a heavy blanket covered what my butt felt to be a deep tear in the seat. I (or, rather, my butt) also felt a rusty coil that protruded out of that tear and, lucky for me, protruded rather placidly in the direction of my left thigh. After hitting a few bumps in the road— which occurred each time we ran over a pebble or a curb—I quickly learned to position myself so the coil would cause minimal pain and I would be able to walk out of the car with all limbs intact. After the first few minutes and a successful exit from the airport, I stopped noticing anything except the night air of New Delhi. It seemed that both of my kids also were noticing the air, as they were wrinkling their noses and incessantly waving their hands in front of their faces to indicate their dissatisfaction with the air.

"Smell your garlands," I hissed at my mortifyingly impolite off-spring, and proceeded to do the same, all the while hoping not to inhale the delicate flower into my nostril through my increasingly acute breaths.

"So these are your children," mused Kamal in the meantime. "How old are they?"

"Twelve and ten."

"Very young, very young," Kamal shook his head in concern. "What is your name, young boy?" he asked, turning his head toward my older son.

"Julian"

"And yours, young girl?"

Kamal was now clearly looking at Fillip, but we were so busy sniffing our flower gardens that we both chose to ignore that little oversight.

"Fillip."

"Ah, that's nice," sighed Kamal. "A boy and a girl."

"A boy and a boy!" I corrected Kamal while Julian snickered loudly at the plight of poor Fillip, who had turned beet-red and was staring at me as if I were the cause of Kamal's confusion. Both Julian and Fillip had long hair. But while Julian's was just a long version of what could potentially be a man's cut, Fillip's hair was pushed to the sides behind both ears and fell in big curls down past his shoulders. In a country where long hair equaled woman and short hair equaled man, Fillip's gender was a natural cause for confusion. Kamal would be the first, but, unfortunately, not the last to be baffled by this enigma of a child.

"What hotel did you reserve, Madame?" Kamal clearly wanted to move beyond his little blunder and start anew what was to be a two-week relationship.

"Shanti Home, Kamal. Do you know it?"

"No, Madame. Do you have an address, perhaps?" Of course I did. Unfortunately, the address meant nothing to Kamal. We soon found out that it meant nothing to the next ten or twelve people we proceeded to stop on various corners and intersections. Phone calls to fellow drivers did not help either. My excitement of driving around the streets of New Delhi wore off after the first forty or fifty minutes. At this point, I just wanted to find our beds for the night and a place where we could at least grab something to eat (as opposed to the full dinner we were planning when we still estimated our hotel arrival to be about eight o'clock). A few more conversations with the hotel staff finally got us on the right road and voila, less than two and a half hours later, we were finally at our hotel, thanks to the bellhop who was asked to stand a block away at the main thoroughfare and look out for our Land Cruiser.

Shanti Home did indeed prove to be a lovely place. We were met with more flower garlands and stares from the staff. I was happy to note that they had received one of the three salwar kameezes I had ordered while still back home; I had known it wasn't going to get to my house in time for the trip, so I had it shipped directly to the hotel. I modeled it for my kids when we got to our room. Their initial stunned silence was finally broken by a loud, obnoxious, and lingering bout of laughter—not the reaction I had expected. The truth is, a number of people on the travel sites back in the States had advised that it's a good idea for female travelers in India to dress in this traditional Indian outfit. A salwar kameez, worn by both men and women, consists of a long tunic and a pair of pants that are usually wide at the top and taper at the bottom. In fact, one of the three outfits I purchased tapered to an opening of no more than two inches, which forced my foot to contort to incredible shapes and took ten to fifteen minutes to just get in or out of. But I was convinced that parading around India in a salwar kameez, albeit one that fit poorly, would allow me to blend in.

"Oh, yeah, Mom, you blend." I was not sure if my kids were crying, laughing, or both. "You have bright red hair with jet black streaks, you're packing heels and are trailed by two boys with long hair. You blend!"

There was no way these two were going to deter me from believing that I would look good and I would blend. I would love every minute of everything that India had to offer, regardless of the two laughing hyenas in my room. So off we were to the rooftop restaurant that our receptionist assured us was still open.

The restaurant actually was open, even if the chef looked like he had just been dragged out of bed kicking and screaming. He assumed an air of contentment, anyway, and asked us what we wanted. It was past eleven o'clock at night. Having a three-course meal followed immediately by bedtime did not appeal to us, so we settled for some *naan,* a traditional Indian oven-baked flat bread that comes plain or stuffed with all sorts of goodies, from potatoes to garlic and onions and anything else a chef can think of sticking inside. Our longtime favorite from the Indian restaurants in New York, the kids and I were perfectly happy ordering a few of these as a meal. Needless to say, the sleepy chef sent a grinning waiter back to our table just to ensure that the three crazy New Yorkers understood that *naan* is just bread; was that really all we wanted? We happily nodded our heads yes and proceeded to sip some red wine. Well, I sipped the red wine. The kids just settled for some iced tea.

The sleepy chef, in the meantime, started to knead the dough and pump it with his fists. I imagined he pictured our faces while doing that. Whatever he may have thought luckily did not pass into the *naans* themselves; they were undoubtedly the best *naans* we ever had. Even today, my mouth waters just thinking about our dinner that first night in New Delhi. Here we were, on a rooftop overlooking the sleeping capital, feeling the comfortingly warm air on our skins, sipping our drinks, and eating *naan,* which we ordered twice more before the night was over. We were finally in India, and we were very happy.

That is, until we went back to our rooms. My suggestion of a shower proved to be a total disaster. The water heater in the tiny bathroom only heated two handfuls of water at a time and only to tepid. The sudden spray of hot water that the feeble showerhead let out as soon it was turned on was nothing more than a tease, followed by a meager stream that alternated between lukewarm and icy cold. Because there was no curtain or even a shower stall, the showerhead sprayed water everywhere, resulting in an inevitable flood in the bathroom and prompting us to shut off the water after the third spray of lukewarm. After a few attempts, we settled for quick run-in, run-out showers and were all too happy to hit the pillow, none of us feeling any more refreshed.

Chapter 3

NEW DELHI

The next morning, I woke up before five o'clock. I tried going back to sleep, but after a few attempts I noticed Fillip staring at me wide-eyed from his pillow.

"How long have you been up?"

"About an hour."

"Did you try going back to sleep?"

"Um, have you?"

"OK, got you, stupid question. Is your brother awake?"

"Yes, he is," lied my little angel as he loudly smacked his brother on top of the head. Poor Julian jolted straight up, trying to figure out what roused him.

"See, told you he's awake," Fillip haughtily grinned.

"Fine," I sighed. "Let's get out of here and go have breakfast."

After climbing three flights of stairs to the rooftop restaurant, we merrily settled in for a breakfast of eggs and toast. To our dismay, both tasted like paper napkins that were used to clean salt off a table-cloth. Still tasting the excitement of last night's *naan*, this was a huge disappointment.

"Look, Mom—a skunk!" Fillip was wildly gesticulating in the direction of the neighboring rooftop.

"A what?"

"A skunk! Didn't you see it? Right there on the other roof."

I'm a city girl; I have never seen a skunk before. I have read about them. I've seen pictures of them. I even remembered one by the name of Pepe Le Pew. But as far as I knew, none of those skunks had been known to climb walls.

"I don't think it was a skunk. I'm sure you saw something else."

"There it is again." Fillip was vehement about the skunk, so Julian and I turned to see…a chipmunk. The tiny rodent was cheer-fully hopping from rooftop to rooftop. Oh well, you know what they say: you can take the boy out of the city, but you can't take the city out of the boy. In the next two weeks, we saw hundreds of "skunks," but the joke never got old.

By ten o'clock in the morning, Kamal was waiting for us outside our hotel. We would first stop at his office, he informed us, to pay the boss, and then we had a full day of sightseeing. I knew climbing into the Land Cruiser that I was not feeling well. I had felt fine when I woke up. I had breakfast, packed, and felt OK until we settled into the car. Then I was overcome by an awful feeling of nausea that started getting worse by the minute. The sights outside the window did not help my condition: windy dusty roads surrounded a bit too closely by mud huts and decrepit plaster structures that looked suspiciously fragile. Everywhere I looked, there were barefoot children wearing long, loose tunics, their faces muddy and their hair dirty and matted. We were far from any tourist areas. This was the heart of New Delhi, and this heart beat to its own pulse.

It is virtually impossible to describe the traffic pattern in any city in India. This is because most of it needs to be smelled, heard, and witnessed to be believed. Even in a large and modern city like New Delhi, any semblance of order was nonexistent beyond the main thoroughfare. There were no traffic lights, no lanes, and no street names. Traffic was one big mass of life: cows, bicycles, rickshaws, cars, mopeds, people, monkeys, goats. There was no rhyme or reason in all this movement, just a lot of noise and commotion. Traffic moved slowly and chaotically. Everything on two or more wheels tooted and beeped incessantly. If it had no wheels, it mooed or bleated. Encompassed by the hazy rays of the muddy, pre-monsoon sun, the whole city blended into one huge organism, which appeared preoccupied with millions of things at once and none in particular.

As fascinated as I was, I was feeling incredibly nauseous when Kamal pulled up in front of a dilapidated old building that looked like something one would see in history books, usually followed by words like "third world" and "seventeenth century."

"We go to the boss, Madame," declared Kamal definitively, and all I could do was to point to the trunk with a palm up sign, which I hoped was universal for "lift." I was afraid that if I opened my mouth to speak I would get sick right there on the sidewalk. There, on top of two carry-on cases, was my makeup bag. My pride and joy, this wheeled black case fit everything a girl needed on a trip: makeup, perfume, various shampoo and conditioner bottles, soaps, lotions, brushes, a hair straightener, a travel iron, and many more items women positively cannot travel without. On this trip, however, this bag had to be stretched to the limit to allow room for medicine. Come to think of it, describing the content of the bag as medicine would not do it justice. This bag was a hospital on wheels. It contained remedies for every disease and injury known to man and some even for ailments not yet discovered. I reached for some nausea pills and swallowed them right there, in the middle of a dusty street, standing between a cow (who I could swear was staring at me) and an overheated Land Cruiser. For just a split second, the thought did cross my mind that I should probably be taking pills in a more sterile environment. But I suspected that very spot was as good an environment as I would get. So I forced down the two caplets and followed Kamal up the stairs of the suspicious-looking office building.

We walked two flights of stairs up to what looked like someone's private apartment. And that's exactly what it was. Here lived Jawahar, the owner of the travel agency, together with his family. In the same apartment, next to a pile of old wooden toys and a tiny niche I identified as a kitchen, was Jawahar's office. The kids and I followed him there. Jawahar kindly offered us three chairs and tea. We accepted the chairs but refused the tea. We were deathly afraid of the potential bacteria in the cups washed in anything less than boiled water. Guidebook after guidebook that we read before leaving home described gruesome agony and torment that awaited any unsuspecting Western traveler in India who did not follow the rules: never drink (or brush your teeth) with anything other than bottled water, do not eat fruits or vegetables that cannot be peeled or were not cooked, wash and sanitize your hands 257 times a day, etc. And this was, after all, our first day in the country. All those rules were still fresh in our minds and we were still under a grand delusion that as long as we could follow them to the letter, we would never experience the misery and distress that all those other, uneducated travelers experienced.

"If I have to use the restroom," I whispered to the kids, "do not get alarmed. I am not feeling very well. I'm fine, but I might need to use the restroom." I looked around, trying to figure out if there was a bathroom inside the apartment, and if there was, would I dare use it? I mean, come on; going into someone's house and heading straight for the bathroom to get sick was not exactly a reflection of good manners.

Jawahar was counting money, explaining something to me, writing down his phone number for emergencies, smiling, and being generally helpful. I hardly understood any of it. I just remember thinking that if I could just get through that morning, I could probably survive anything. Before I knew it, we were walking out, and then we were outside, getting back into our bony Land Cruiser. The pills must have worked, because I started to feel better, and my nausea, although it did not disappear completely, subsided and took second place to the excitement of being in India.

We were finally on the way to see something. Kamal diligently tried explaining to us where we were going and what we were about to see. After each explanation, the kids turned to me and inquired in unison: "What did he say?" Either my Hindi was not good or his English was not clear, but all I could do in response was shrug my shoulders and leaf through the guidebook.

Our first stop was Humayun's tomb. Built in the sixteenth century, this tomb complex houses graves of the Mughal Emperor Humayun, his wife Hamida Begum, Dara Shikoh (son of the later Emperor Shah Jahan), and numerous other subsequent Mughals.

Kamal let us out in front of the complex and waved in the general direction of the entrance. Not too many people travel to India at the end of April; the oppressively hot air keeps away all but the most dedicated tourists, so the entrance to the ticket booth was quite empty. We happily paid our $5 and were about to walk through the turnstile, the last frontier between us and the tomb complex. This seemed to not have sat well with the cashier, who suddenly shrieked and proceeded to try to tell us something, all the while wildly gesticulating and pointing intermittently at us and something to our right. In all this agitation, he seemed to have forgotten the twenty English words he had displayed knowledge of prior to that. All we could understand from the loud pantomime was that we were not to walk through the turnstile. We looked around to see if perhaps there was a different entry into the complex, but there was not. We were very perplexed. I tried to have another conversation with the cashier when an older Indian couple got in line behind us.

"You need to give ticket to man," the husband helpfully offered.

"What man, the cashier?" The cashier was the only man I saw, so the older gentleman's comment only confused me further.

"No, the other man," clarified my helper, leaving me just as confused as before.

Then I saw him. From the corner of my eye, I spotted a middle-aged gentleman moving toward us. He was wearing some kind of an official uniform topped with a beret playfully placed so far down the left side of his temple that he had to keep his head tilted to the right just to keep it from falling. That, coupled with the fact that he was eating something resembling nuts or seeds and spitting shells in both directions, clearly slowed his walking speed. As a result, it took him about three minutes more to reach us and take his rightful place next to the turnstiles, which were located right next to the cashier's booth. The beret-clad gentleman, taking his job very seriously, carefully examined the tickets before making a small tear at the top. It was only then, after all the proper procedures were observed, that we were able to make our entry into the tomb complex.

The tomb did not disappoint. It was a huge, mostly empty compound with beautiful red-brick structures that took our breath away. We passed one crypt after the other, until we arrived at the gate of the main mausoleum, which bore an uncanny resemblance to the Taj Mahal. I was awestruck. Julian was captivated, as well. But there was something about this majestic structure that really struck a chord with Fillip. The place completely enthralled him. Julian and I spent hours running after him into every crevice and cranny as he examined every inch of that glorious landmark. The child was in seventh heaven; so was I.

After a few hours of euphoria, we were ready for lunch. Well, the kids were ready for lunch. I was still feeling a bit nauseous, so although I was slightly hungry, the thought of food scared me.

"Kamal, can we find a place for lunch?" Kamal was waiting for us outside, talking with other drivers who, likewise, were waiting for their passengers, whom we had not even noticed in the vast tomb complex.

"Yes, Madame, there is a nice place I can take you that is very near."

"Sounds good, Kamal. We trust your judgment."

The place Kamal had in mind was very close indeed. It was in what looked like a residential neighborhood that we probably would never think to visit. It was tucked away in a corner of what almost looked like a typical American mini-mall, with a pharmacy on one end and a toy store on the other. There was only one minor detail that served as reminder that this, after all, was India: a snake charmer. He sat cross-legged, strategically positioned in front of the toy store and diligently enticed all passersby to take photos with him and his lovely assistant king cobra. Luckily for me, the kids were too hungry to pause in front of the eccentric duo, so with a mere promise of stopping there on the way back, we proceeded to the restaurant.

Kamal walked us to the door, pointed toward the entrance and told us he would wait for us in the car. At the door, a rather large Sikh man wearing a colorful turban, which somehow seemed like a perfect complement to his dark blue doorman's uniform, greeted us. There was something about the way he was examining potential customers that threw me right back to childhood. It was long ago, as a child in Soviet Russia, that I witnessed doormen treating foreigners with lackey-like veneration while tossing aside—sometimes physically—the citizens of their own country. Tourists could go into the best restaurants (some of which actually carried a sign outside advising people that the establishment was not for the Soviet citizens), exclusive nightclubs, and shops. Some of those privileges were, likewise, reserved for the Soviet elite. In a country that proclaimed equality for all, this blatant hypocrisy was revolting, to say the least. So here I was, many years later, in India, witnessing the same from a doorman in a tucked away restaurant in New Delhi. The same man who was all too attentive to us and the noticeably well-to-do Indian visitors barked something rude under his breath toward every local who looked like he, too, might wish to partake in the offerings of the establishment. But faced with the choice between class revolt and protest and feeding my own hungry children, I have to admit, with shame, that I settled for the latter.

Once inside, the restaurant showed little promise. It looked like a strange eclectic mixture of a New York Chinese restaurant and a 1980s disco. Hosts in suits, circa 1982, greeted visitors at the door and escorted them to one of many dark redwood and faux-leather booths. The menu was in English, and even the dishes with the more exotic-sounding names had disappointingly prosaic descriptions like "'rice with peas" or "lentils in sauce." After lengthy deliberations, the kids finally settled on the chicken curry, while I refused to chance eating anything other than plain saffron rice, albeit with some white wine (nauseous or not, a girl needs a beverage). The place was not very busy. Most of the people there were tourists, like us, although scattered among them were some locals. Dressed in bright colors and expensive fabrics, these were mostly well-to-do families sharing an afternoon meal or an occasional dating couple chatting and giggling over their meal. Unlike us, even the younger couples did not avail themselves of the services of utensils; all food was eaten with the help of a *naan* or *roti* bread. Both were flat and thin enough to bend and scoop the food like a giant spoon. I imagined my unskillful fingers trying to perform the same feat and could visualize the sight of brown lentils against a pale turquoise blouse. After some consideration, I decided to stick with a fork and knife.

When we left the restaurant, the sun was too hot and the kids too full and sedate to insist on stopping in front of the snake charmer. Not to appear that they were letting me off the hook, the kids nonetheless did nod in that general direction and murmured something about promises, inexpensive thrills, and something else along those lines. I was able to quickly dismiss them with just a wave of the hand and move hurriedly toward the Land Cruiser.

The second part of our day did not impress us in the same way Humayun's tomb did. To be sure, the Red Fort is a glorious sight. In the seventeenth century, when Shah Jahan moved the Mughal Empire's capital from Agra to Delhi, he built this magnificent complex of a palace and fortifications, constructed almost entirely of the red brick that gives the site its name. Today, the fortification walls are perfectly intact. The grounds of the complex are well landscaped and dreamy and, surrounded by the tall rampart walls, give the whole place a very pensive, almost romantic feel. Perhaps that was the reason why, once inside the fort, we found ourselves in what seemed to be a mating ground for teenaged and twenty-something locals. Everywhere we looked, we saw couples in various stages of embrace, some leaning against palm trees, others on the ground propped up against the palace walls. Some of them made this mother of two prepubescent boys very uncomfortable (and it takes a lot to make me uncomfortable). Luckily for me, after the fifth or sixth such scene, my ten-year-old saw another "skunk", and we spent the rest of our time at the Red Fort chasing chipmunks that were chasing each other. Perhaps if the fort had been our first sightseeing stop that day, we would have truly appreciated it. Unfortunately, Humayun's tomb was too tough an act to follow.

"Madame, I take you to train station now," declared Kamal as soon as we climbed back into the Land Cruiser. "Station very crowded at this time; we need to go early."

"That's fine, Kamal; train station it is."

We had train tickets reserved for the night train to Varanasi. When I was growing up, train travel was the most popular means of transportation in Europe. Families would regularly spend days—if not weeks—traversing the vast terrains of the Soviet Union. Flights were scarce and prices exorbitant. Trains, on the other hand, were numerous and relatively cheap. As a child, I loved trains. The top bunk was always reserved for me, and I would spend hours on the second level of the sleeper berth looking through the small, mud-covered top part of the window. The room would always smell of roasted chicken, as my mother could hardly wait to get on the train before unloading the numerous bags of food she had packed for the road. Train restaurants were too expensive and limited in their selection, so people packed food that could last without much refrigeration: smoked sausages, hard-boiled eggs, roasted chicken, vegetables, fruits, bread, etc. Somehow, cold roasted chicken never tasted as good as when eaten on the top berth of a train.

The year before coming to India, I had tried to recreate that experience for my children when we took a night train from Vienna to Cologne—minus the roasted chicken; I was on vacation, after all, and I did not know how to order roasted chicken in a deli. Everything about that night was magical for us: the kids' first night train, dinner consisting of freshly baked bread, smoked sausages, vegetables, various spreads and red wine (well, juice for the kids, I think, but I remember the wine), meticulously clean bed sheets, and carpeting that was vacuumed to such perfection that we could've eaten off of it. Needless to say, we could not wait to relive that experience in India. But this was Planet India, and everything here was a world away from what we knew as civilization.

The train station looked like one giant vortex of activity. It was crowded well above maximum capacity. As far as the eye could see, there were bodies: human bodies, cow bodies, goat bodies, crippled-to-obscenity beggar bodies, tall red-turbaned porter bodies, gray-clad station worker bodies, crying children bodies, old people bodies, blind bodies, rich bejeweled bodies, and other bodies that defied description. This solid mass of activity looked frenzied, chaotic, and impenetrable. It was coming, going, grazing, jumping, running, begging, peddling, selling, greeting, carrying, pushing, shoving, yelling, waving arms, and hauling bags. The hustle and bustle of hundreds of thousands of beings spilled out from narrow platforms onto the tracks. Train arrivals were accompanied by loud whistles that somehow resembled cow moos. The moo-whistles forced creatures to casually change tracks and proceed in the same fashion on the next track until another train-moo sent them scurrying to yet another track, so they zigzagged the tracks until some final purpose made them climb onto the platform and disappear into the station vortex.

My initial reaction was panic. How was I, accompanied by two children and luggage, going to traverse this unruly mess and actually find our train? Kamal read my mind. "Wait here, Madame. I will find porter." He did not have to ask us twice. Both kids and I remained as if glued to the side of the Land Cruiser. The sight of the train station bedlam left us motionless and we were more than happy to have Kamal see us out of this mayhem.

Kamal quickly reappeared, accompanied by a porter. The porter was short and boney, with dark, wrinkled skin. He looked like he was in his sixties or seventies and had not had a meal in the last four months. This was to be our guide and guardian until the train left the station. In loud Hindi, Kamal proceeded to negotiate the price with the porter, intermittently pointing to the kids, the luggage, and me. They finally agreed to forty-five rupees—less than one U.S. dollar— and I was more than happy to consent.

"Madame, I will drive and meet you in Khajuraho," Kamal reminded me as we said our good-byes. Though we would have a different driver in Varanasi, Kamal was going to drive the Land Cruiser straight to Khajuraho, our next destination, and accompany us for the next fourteen days in Rajasthan.

I turned to the porter, who, with a wide, toothless grin, threw both of our suitcases on top of his red turban. "Wow," the kids said in unison, as he wrestled from them our trusted makeup case and masterfully holstered it around his shoulder. He motioned for us to follow him, which we gladly did, as he made a passageway through the station vortex, through the beggars and the peddlers, through the goats and the children. This old skinny porter, balancing two suitcases on his head and another on his shoulder, became our own private Moses. Supporting the suitcases with one hand, he waved the free hand as a cane in front of him. And just as Moses thrust his staff to part the waters of the Red Sea, our porter used his bony palm, not unlike the blade of an oar—left, right, left, right—to propel numerous bodies to the left or to the right with every wave. And like the waves of the sea, the bodies parted, almost mechanically and without much thought, to pave the path for our porter and us in tow. He finally brought us to what we hoped was our platform, set down our luggage, and with a wide, toothless *namaste* (which means good day, but literally translates to "the divinity in me bows to the divinity in you") disappeared into the crowd.

We found ourselves standing on a narrow concrete platform next to a seemingly affluent Indian couple in their fifties. The wife, dressed in a bright yellow sari, sat on a huge soft suitcase surrounded by about five or six bags that were just as large and bulging as her husband's stomach. She kept fanning herself with a look of utter disinterest, as the husband, a dark, balding gentleman with a thick gold chain around his neck and chunky rings on both of his pinkies, kept lecturing her on something in a hushed monotonous voice.

"Varanasi?" I asked, pointing in the general direction of the tracks on which I was hoping the train would appear soon.

"Varanasi," answered the husband, and without missing a beat he continued his lecture.

Waiting on the platform made the kids and me stationary targets for every peddler and beggar of the station vortex. In the ten or so minutes that it took for the train to pull into the station with a loud moo-whistle, we were approached by one man without legs, pulling his body along the ground on his knuckles, four children aged between four and six with their hands out, repeating "Madame, Madame" and shaking their open little palms at me, an old blind woman dressed in rags and walking with the aid of a broken cane that was held together by pieces of blue duct tape, and numerous peddlers offering us everything from water to pastries to jewelry to toys. It is very difficult to be objective about poverty in India. Poverty in India is everywhere; it is part of the Indian landscape. Coming from the West, where our aspiration is to help everyone worse off than us, it is quite hard to realize that we cannot possibly help every destitute person in India. It is heartbreaking to see children with deformities, old people with their hands out, and cripples reduced to crawling on the floor for lack of medicine or technology available to them. And so, with a polite wave of the hand, we dismiss them, often doing so a few times until they finally understand that we will not give them anything, and they crawl away.

My happiness at the sight of the train was marred only by the conductor, who, upon exiting, locked up the entrance and was immediately swallowed up by the station vortex. We had forty minutes before the train's departure. I knew we were going to spend all of it on the platform, fending off more unfortunates and catching displeased glances from the Indian couple waiting next to us. After all, the beggars were attracted to us because we stood out, but once they approached us, it was very easy for them to spot the woman and her gem-adorned husband. Thus, because of us, our soon-to-be train neighbors became the focus of the same beggars and peddlers. Needless to say, there was not going to be any friendship developing between us anytime soon.

Finally, five minutes before train departure, the conductor returned. He silently took our tickets, compared our names to his passenger roster, and waved us unto the train. The Indian couple who went ahead of us had four porters carrying the numerous bags they had with them. Within minutes, their bags were on the train, safely tucked away among the crevices of the storage compartment next to their sleeper. We, on the other hand, had dismissed our porter long ago. Having to carry suitcases onto what turned out to be a very high train step was an undertaking all on its own. Finding our sleeper was another undertaking, as the conductor looked rather irritated by our lack of train experience and instead of offering help, stood aside and monitored our frustration with disdain.

A year before, when buying a train ticket in Vienna, I found out that sleeping compartments usually have four berths. Anyone purchasing a berth was allocated the first vacant space in any sleeper. Therefore, in order to ensure privacy, I had purchased an extra ticket, and the kids and I had a vacant bed and enjoyed a compartment all to ourselves. This was not the case in India. When I shared my plans with Jawahar, he kindly advised me to save my money. *"Ye hai India,* darling," he declared with an apologetic shrug. "This is India, darling. Learn to say it, and you'll be fine. You can buy as many sleeping berths as you wish, but when the train conductor notices that a passenger did not board at any given station, he will sell that berth before you even have a chance to lock the door. Do not even bother explaining to him about privacy. *Ye hai India,* darling. Don't waste your money!"

So there we were, a year later, looking for the sleep compartment that we were going to share with a stranger. I braced myself for the worst. I envisioned someone resembling our next–door neighbor, who wore 1970s wide-collar shirts, had an enormous gut, and adorned himself with enough gold and jewels to feed a family of four for a year. The best I could hope for was lack of body odor, a smell that had plagued us ever since we entered the train station. The only thing that occasionally replaced the smell of body odor was the smell of cologne, which was applied in such copious amounts that it sent my nose into shock and made me wish I had a severe cold.

I was so concerned about sharing a sleeper with a stranger that I didn't stop to think about what a room would be like. Not wanting to take any chances, I had booked a first-class compartment. The accommodations were as good as any Indian train had to offer, yet still cheap enough by Western standards. It was going to be an air-conditioned lap of luxury. I'm not sure if I really believed that, but I did expect something vaguely resembling our Vienna experience. The compartment we found ourselves in was nothing of the sort. It was a grim affair, consisting of four sleeping spaces—two couches that turned into beds before nighttime and two upper berths designed as hanging beds on top of the couches. All four looked old and worn out, just like the rest of the train, which had peeling paint and mud-covered windows from many years of use and very little care. But without a doubt, the bed sheets took the prize for highest shock value. The sheets on each of our beds had huge brown stains on them from sources I did not care to identify. I frantically searched for the conductor call button. It took me a few bangs on the button to realize it was not working, so off I went, at the risk of further annoying our conductor.

"Yes, Madame." He did not even try to feign a smile at my approach.

"Excuse me, sir. Can you please have our sheets changed? They seem to have some stains on them."

"I will see," he said and followed me into the room.

I displayed all the sheets to the conductor, hoping to see some sympathy and a resolve to fix the situation. Instead of sympathy, the conductor's reaction was even more disdain. He took away the sheets and left the compartment without saying anything else. I hoped for the best. My hopes were shattered when he returned five minutes later with new sheets. I am not sure if he just refolded the old sheets or really brought new ones, but I could see no difference; the stains were still there. Fillip burst out laughing. I shot him a stern look and proceeded to explain to the conductor that I wanted him to exchange the sheets because we really would prefer to have sheets without stains. Once again, the conductor silently took the sheets and left. After repeating this exercise about four more times, we finally gave up. Either the train did not carry sheets without stains or our conductor was some kind of a sadist who wanted to see how long it would be before I began to cry. Fat chance. *Ye hai India.* We were going to have to spend a night on dirty sheets.

In all this commotion, we had hardly noticed the tall gentleman with black curly hair who quietly walked into the compartment and sat down on the bottom berth across from mine. He watched in silent

bewilderment as our sheet saga unfolded. He clearly did not understand what the big deal was and why it was worth it for us to continue tormenting this poor, hardworking conductor. I decided not to
pursue the subject with him. Clearly, he was not on our side in this
little drama.

Rakesh was a thin man in his late thirties. He wore old-fashioned
brown-rimmed round glasses that matched his dated brown corduroy
jacket. Rakesh looked sad even while smiling. He was a physician
going back to work in Varanasi after visiting relatives in New Delhi.
His English was good enough and we chatted quite a while about
his life in India, his work, and his ambitions. Rakesh told me how
much he loved being a doctor; medicine was a true calling and a life's
dream. He also told me how much he loved India but how desperately he wanted to leave it. Compared to Western standards, doctors
do not earn much money in India. Most of them work in national
clinics that are government sponsored and do not pay much. The
only money doctors hoped to make was working in a private practice.
Unfortunately, there were not too many of those, as the majority of
Indian people could not afford their fees and trying to find those who
could was a huge marketing undertaking, which Rakesh could not or
would not do.

His only hope was to find a job abroad. He did not particularly
care which country; if there was an opening, Rakesh was willing to
explore it. At least he would live in an apartment that always had
running water and electricity and where gas was a standard feature,
as opposed to an item one had to stock up on. Even though Rakesh's
apartment building was considered new and modern, it lacked most
of the standard facilities that we in the West were accustomed to.
In fact, even something simple like a shower stall was missing in a

typical Indian bathroom. Furthermore, the small water heater hanging in the bathroom heated barely enough water to wash one's hair; anything more than that had to be done with cold water. Yet Rakesh considered himself lucky; many of his neighbors still did not have facilities inside the flat and had to go down the hall—or worse, down to the rail tracks—to take care of their bodily functions. Rakesh had a love-hate relationship with India. He loved his country; he loved its customs, its holy places, and its traditions. But he hated the fact that the country was pushing him out; by not providing for him, the country declared him unimportant. India did not want Rakesh the way Rakesh wanted India. It did not care if he stayed or went, and it made Rakesh furious—well, as furious as this gentleman in brown could get.

While Rakesh and I continued chatting, the kids were helping themselves to the sandwiches we had brought with us for dinner. Not trusting Indian train food (or any country's train food, for that matter), I believed the only way to have dinner on a night train was in our compartment. Before driving us to the station, Kamal had stopped in a small shop resembling any midtown New York eatery where sandwiches were prepared hours in advance of one's order and the décor was as tired as the red-yellow uniforms worn by the staff, who looked like a bunch of frazzled twelve-year-olds. The sandwiches tasted as dreadful as they looked. The kids wearily chewed on some cold meat wedged between two pieces of Western-style stale bread while I struggled through *dal* on white, a miserable combination of spicy and drab. I offered some to Rakesh. He, however, unaware of the train-food taboo, looked quite happy sweeping up his train-purchased *dal* with his train-purchased *roti* bread. The food was sold by a *wallah*, or vendor, carrying huge trays of it from car to car. Watching Rakesh devour his dinner with such zeal, I reconsidered our own train-dinner options, but before I had a chance to change my mind, the *wallah* was gone. Chasing a food *wallah* from car to car did not appeal to my children or me so we just settled for our earlier choices and waited impatiently for the *chai-wallah* to appear.

It did not take long for the smell of *masala chai* to hit our nostrils. We smelled it before we heard the *chai-wallah* announcing his goods from the other end of the train-car. *Masala chai* would become the beverage of choice for my older son, Julian, who to this very day drinks it every chance he gets. In India, however, more than anywhere else in the world, *masala chai* is an unrivaled art form that is learned in childhood. It is made by brewing tea with a mixture of Indian herbs and spices. This combination is boiled together with milk and served piping hot, after the *chai-wallah* skillfully pours it from the pot, which he holds at the height of his fully extended arm into a cup he holds as low as his other arm can drop. Every time I saw these chai performances in India, I marveled at the *wallah's* ability to transfer scalding-hot liquid from one container to another with maximum aplomb and minimum casualties.

After dinner, I sent the kids off to the bathroom armed with toothbrushes and bottled water and wondered how I would be able to wash up in a tiny train bathroom that kept jumping up in sync with a moving train. Never denying myself an evening routine of removing makeup and applying all kinds of toners, serums, lotions, creams, I decided to limit myself to a twenty-minute procedure with a mirror and my makeup case right there in my compartment on top of the bottom berth. All the while, polite Rakesh tried very hard to pretend he was not looking. I kept thinking how funny the story of a crazed woman who kept pulling bottles out of a huge case would sound when Rakesh told his friends in the morning. The story became even funnier when the kids returned. Julian showed me how filthy his feet were after a day of traversing New Delhi's dusty streets. Never without a solution, I produced an oversized moist wipe from my case. I had bought these "body wipes" before our trip, thinking there might be a day when water was not available, making the pounds of soap packed into our case totally useless. This was such a case. The body wipe, however, was no match for New Delhi's dirt. After about thirty minutes and four towels, I suggested that he just give up.

"I hate going to bed with dirty feet," declared my twelve-year-old. I was impressed that my hygiene sermons had taken hold. However, after such a lengthy battle with dirt, we simply had to admit defeat and retreat. Dirt won, and we needed sleep. So, for the first time in his conscious life, Julian went to bed with dirty feet.

Both kids were dead asleep within ten minutes. I, however, lost two more battles that night. The first one was with the faucet of the bathroom sink; it refused to cooperate, and all my prodding and twisting and poking and pleading did not produce more than two sorry drops of water. The second battle was lost before it began. I had taken one look at the train toilet and decided that my next bathroom break would have to wait until we got off the train. I was not sure our hotel bathroom would be any cleaner, but I could not imagine it looking or smelling any worse.

Chapter 4

VARANASI

There was only one difference between the train station in New Delhi and the train station in Varanasi: size. The new station to which we pulled up early the following morning was a miniature version of the one we had left from. It was the same chaotic vortex, except a bit smaller. The living mass covered the horizon, which included exits to the street and various signs, most of which were so faded that they could not be read anyway. Not knowing which way to start walking to meet our driver for the next two days, we decided to stay put and let the vortex dissolve with the departing train. I was hoping that the sight of a redheaded woman with two longhaired boys would attract our driver to us and we would be on our way. Ten minutes later, the vortex had almost entirely disappeared, leaving the three of us standing alone on the platform leaning against our luggage. There was no sign of the driver. As a matter of fact, there was no sign of anyone vaguely resembling a driver. I looked up Jawahar's phone number, but it was one thing to find the phone number and another to dial it. It would take me another ten or fifteen minutes to finally figure out which set of numbers to press from my U.S.-based cell phone to correctly dial New Delhi. I was very relieved to hear that the driver did not forget about us; he was on his way and would be meeting us shortly.

"Why don't you start walking to exit?" Jawahar screamed on the other side of the phone.

"Because there are about twenty signs and they are all pointing in different directions," I replied, just as loudly, partly due to the background noise and partly out of frustration.

"All right, then. If you prefer, just stay there and wait for the driver," Jawahar shouted.

Another ten minutes passed, and finally I spotted a balding little man with a huge toothless grin. He carefully examined the kids and me before revealing a sign: "Madame Magolez." By that time, I remembered that my name had become Magolez, so I waved and led the kids in his direction.

"*Namaste*, Madame," said the toothless man as he reached for our luggage.

"*Namaste*, sir," I answered. "I am Mariann. What is your name?" What followed next was an awkward session of questions and answers resulting in absolutely nothing. We would spend the next two days with this kind man, whose name we were never able to understand.

"Hotel?" asked the toothless man, and I reached into my bag to produce travel documents.

"Hotel Palace On The River," I read, and off we went in his little Toyota sedan. The car was small and comfortable enough for just the three of us and we were very happy to find it air-conditioned, as the heat outside neared 40°C.

We drove through what looked like the outskirts of the city. Newer buildings and structures resembling schools and government offices were part of the horizon, blending into an already-familiar throng of people and livestock. And then we drove into the center of Varanasi. At first glance it seemed to us even more crowded than the center of New Delhi, if that was even possible. After driving—or rather carefully crawling—into what looked like a main intersection, we came to a roadblock. Our toothless driver opened the window of our air-conditioned car and shouted something at the driver of a rickshaw next to us. The rickshaw driver shrugged his shoulders, shouted something in return, and pointed his hands in two opposite directions.

"If he just provided us with directions," I thought, "they will be looking for our bodies for many years to come." After a number of honks and break slams, our driver turned the car around and drove into yet another current of pedestrians, peddlers, cows, and goats. About ten minutes and two more conversations between our driver and his fellow taximen later, we found ourselves right back at the closed main street intersection. This time, our driver found a policeman, and another furor ensued, accompanied by shoulder shrugging and arm waving. We finally got off the main drag and our driver parked the car. I looked around for a sign of our hotel, but it was to no avail. We were parked on a tiny street full of small shops selling everything from underwear to hardware. I turned to the driver and shrugged my shoulders with arms outstretched and palms facing up in a universal gesture for "I am confused."

What ensued was pantomiming that cannot be described in words; it involved a number of combinations of sounds and hand gestures exchanged between me and the driver, in addition to useless input from a few passersby with lots of time on their hands. In the end, we somehow understood that we could not go any further. Therefore, the kids and I, along with our luggage, would ride a rickshaw to the hotel and our driver would walk alongside us. Momentarily, there was a rickshaw next to us, but the kids and I examined it with much hesitation; it looked just big enough to comfortably seat one adult. Was this tiny glorified bicycle really going to accommodate two kids, two suitcases, the infamous makeup bag, and me?

Fortunately, we did not have much time for deliberations. Before any of us could protest, the price was negotiated at sixty-five rupees (about $1.25), suitcases were piled behind the seat, and the kids were firmly placed on the rickshaw bench. I had no choice but to place myself next to the kids, balancing my body on my right hip while leaning almost across the kids and supporting myself with just my right arm gripping the back of the bench. Julian, who sat on the opposite side, held my left arm so that I didn't tumble onto the street on the first turn.

Because the streets of Varanasi were more crowded than New York at rush hour during Christmas season, it was no effort for our walking driver to keep up with the rickshaw. As a matter of fact, after strolling leisurely alongside us for a while, he got impatient and walked so far ahead of us that I started to worry that we had lost him forever. My worries were relieved when I saw him at the end of the street, negotiating our next passage. It turned out that the rickshaw took us as far he could and we would have to navigate the rest of the way on foot. When we pulled up at our stop, our driver was having a heated discussion with a few men drinking tea at the end of the street. Not understanding the conversation and not sure what to do next, the kids and I just stood there, surrounded by luggage and the quickly gathered local gentry, curiously examining us and our belongings.

"OK, Madame. Wait here," our driver declared as he disappeared into the crowd. Within seconds, we were surrounded by a sea of people. Some were beggars with outstretched hands, others peddled their wares, and still others were just there because it was the most interesting place to be at that moment. The kids and I tried to look as natural as any human being can while surrounded by a crowd of pointed fingers. Julian and I tried carrying on some small talk. Fillip was not so casual, however.

"They are staring at me," he hissed under his breath.

"They are staring at me too," I hissed back, covering my hiss with a huge smile.

"Why aren't we going to our hotel?"

"Not sure," I said from the corner of my mouth. "We're waiting for our driver."

After what seemed like an eternity, the driver appeared, accompanied by a porter. The porter, a young scrawny man in his twenties, quickly gathered our suitcases and waved for us to follow him, and we were more than happy to oblige. Our driver was right behind us. A few steps away from the main drag, we were swallowed by a wall of houses that stood so close together that the tiny unpaved streets between them were barely enough for two people to cross each other without having to pin themselves against the walls. The smell of the street was unbearable. There was hardly any air reaching the tiny crevices between the buildings, and whatever refuse that had been thrown (or thrown up) into the street remained there, rotting in the hot April air. The stench of garbage, coupled with livestock and their feces and topped with body odor of hundreds of people rushing up and down the tiny streets, created an air so oppressive that I could actually feel it climbing up my nostrils and beating me down with its immensity. The kids immediately started making faces at me and gesturing their disgust at the foul odor. I gestured back by throwing my head in the direction of our driver and pressing my finger against my mouth, motioning them to stop complaining for the sake of our hosts. In compliance, the kids stopped covering their noses but continued to roll their eyes at me, while I tried to visualize tulips to keep my mind off the awful stench.

"Oh my God," Julian, who was walking ahead of me, shrieked so loudly that I jumped and ran ahead, thoroughly scared. As soon as I turned the corner, however, both the stench and the worry gave way to a bout of hysterical laughter. There, around the corner, was my brave son Julian, with his back against the wall, eyes bulging, and mouth gaping wide open. The cause of his fright was a bull. Granted, this bull was rather large and menacing looking. However, his demeanor was so opposite of menacing that Fillip and I could not stop laughing. The bull looked totally disinterested in any life around him. His face looked especially lethargic and almost disdainful. His pace was so slow that it actually came to a halt every few steps and the bull would look up, realize he was not moving, and with great reluctance, attempt to move again. By the time of our departure from Varanasi, this bull became part of our landscape, as we would periodically see him wandering around the *ghats* (the steps leading down to the river).

We followed our driver to the steps of the Manmandir Ghat. There, at the top of the stairs, was our hotel, River Palace. We found our luggage stacked neatly in front of the reception desk. The sight of the suitcases reminded me that I had not paid the porter, whom I noticed standing at the bottom of the hotel stairs.

"I will be right back, sir," I announced to the concierge. "I just need to pay the porter."

I was not sure what about that statement threw our concierge into a frenzy. Although he was still wearing the oversized grin he had assumed upon our arrival, his face promptly turned red and he became visibly uncomfortable.

"Yes, yes, Madame. Please just leave money with us, we give to porter."

Before I had a chance to protest, a bellhop, who seemed to have appeared out of the blue, was speeding off with the money that only a second ago I had in my hand. Almost instinctively, I looked behind me to ensure the money found its rightful destination. I hope it did, as I only saw the back of the porter hurriedly walking back in the direction we had come from.

While the concierge was processing our papers, I waited for our driver to make arrangements for the next day. The driver, in the meantime, was chatting with a man in a pristinely ironed dark blue shirt. He finally walked in and instead of setting the time for tomorrow asked, "Boat river, want, Madame?"

"Very much want!" I responded happily. I had planned to hire a boat anyway and the fact that someone would make these arrangements for me made me happy to deal with one less issue.

"Good, Madame," our driver happily responded. "This man take."

"When?"

"Good on Ganga at sunset and sunrise. So he will take you five o'clock, Madame. Tomorrow, he will take you five thirty. Be here."

"How much will it cost us?"

"One thousand rupees, Madame. Very good price, very good," the driver quickly responded before I even had a chance to object. After doing some quick math in my head, I realized the price amounted to a mere $22, which seemed pretty reasonable to me.

"Fine." The second the word escaped my mouth, I knew this was an outrageously high price by local standards judging by the beaming faces of both the driver and our boatman-to-be. But by that time, both the kids and I were so looking forward to taking a shower and getting out to see Varanasi that any further conversation was unthinkable.

Our hotel room was on the fourth floor of a five-floor walk-up, topped only by the restaurant, whose deck was located right above our room. The first thing that we saw walking into the room was the river. Right in front of our huge stain-filled window, there it was, in all its majesty: the Ganges. The holy *Ganga.* I gasped as I took in the glory of this view. I let out a second gasp after I turned away from the window and looked at our bed; placed neatly on the bed were three white bath towels bearing huge brown stains. As the bellhop was gone by that time, I searched for the phone to call the front desk.

"Hello, this is room 405. Can you please send us up some towels? Ours seem to be dirty."

"What's wrong with your towels?"

Unsure whether the concierge did not hear or did not understand my request, I repeated, "Our towels are dirty; there are brown stains on them. Can you please send some clean ones instead?"

"Yes, Madame."

While waiting for the towels, I decided to examine the bathroom. The sight of the washroom of the Palace on the River almost made me cry. It was neither palatial nor even adequate. I am not sure what was more filthy, the bathtub or the toilet, but the competition was definitely fierce. Both the tub and the toilet featured rusty brown stains. The sink bore yellow marks and numerous scratches both at the bottom and the top of the basin.

"*Ye hai India,* darling," I sighed and rushed to open the door for what I was sure would be three clean towels.

"Madame," began the same bellhop who had shown us to our room fifteen minutes earlier. He was empty-handed.

What ensued was a sequel to our previous train sheet fiasco. The bellhop carefully examined the towels, scrutinized the stains that I pointed out to him, and disappeared. He came back about fifteen minutes later with new towels that contained stains that were, albeit smaller than the previous ones, more numerous. I asked, once again, for these to be changed. The bellhop, once again, disappeared for another fifteen minutes, just to come back with towels whose stains rivaled the ones we previously discarded. By the fourth set of towels, when I could swear I could recognize the stains as those from the first set, we finally accepted that we would have to take showers in a dirty tub and dry ourselves with dirty towels. I knew that no matter how many more times we sent away the poor bellhop, he would still come back with stained towels, simply because those were the only ones available at the hotel.

So, after a really quick cold shower, the kids and I finally left the room. By that time it was almost ten o'clock in the morning and we were very happy to find the hotel restaurant still serving breakfast. We made our way to the fifth floor and took a table inside; although some tables were set up on the outside patio overlooking the Ganges, the early morning sun was already too hot to enjoy. Clearly, Palace on the River was a hotel servicing tourists: the kids were very happy to see pancakes and waffles on the menu, while I settled on an omelet. The waiter brought us utensils, another sign of Western influence. I cheerfully unrolled my cloth napkin just to discover it matched my bath towels: yellow hue with brownish stains. But even my mention of it threw the kids into a panic mode.

"Mom, it's OK. If you start asking for new stuff, we won't see food for another forty minutes. We're really hungry. So the knives are dirty...and the forks. It's fine. We'll live."

I sighed. The kids were absolutely right. Asking for clean napkins or silverware would surely be an exercise in futility, so I resigned myself to eating with dirty utensils, although I could not resist wiping them first with my yellowing napkin. Sadly, the food was no consolation when it arrived. Eggs, I found out, are not something Indians normally eat for breakfast. Therefore, when they do make them, it is usually to cater to foreigners. However, because of many foreigners' distaste for the amount of spice in Indian food, hardly any spices are used when making eggs. I would venture to say none at all are used, so a regular omelet in an Indian hotel tastes as good as that yellowing napkin I had on my lap. It would take a large amount of salt and pepper to revive a lifeless omelet. *Ye hai India.*

Our driver was waiting for us in the same place where he had parked the car earlier. Because we had no luggage we easily traced our way back on foot through the narrow maze off the Ganges and onto the main market street. We were happy to spot the little Toyota around the corner and off we went. Our fist stop that morning was in Sarnath. About ten kilometers from Varanasi, Sarnath is one of the major Buddhist pilgrimage sites. It was here that Buddha chose to deliver his first sermon after attaining enlightenment in 528 BCE. The main shrine in the complex marks the place where Buddha meditated, so we headed straight for the beautiful coned cupola before us.

It took us some time to figure out that shoes are not to be deposited in front of the door. In a country like India, shoes are a commodity to be guarded. Therefore, in front of many temple entrances shoes were checked in, not unlike coats at the Metropolitan Opera. An attendant would take visitors' shoes, give them a numbered tag (most often in a form of a piece of cardboard with a number written in marker), and deposit the shoes into numerous wire cubes placed on top of each other. At the exit, visitors either paid the price listed in front of this service or tipped the attendant if no price was listed. While we were figuring this out, the temple closed for prayer, and we had to wait thirty minutes until it would reopen again for visitors. We retrieved our shoes after paying two rupees (about four cents) and went to explore the beautiful complex grounds, which included the Dhamek Stupa. Built in 500 CE, the Dhamek Stupa is said to mark the very spot where that first Buddha sermon was delivered to his five disciples. It is a cylindrical structure of brown brick and stone covered with exquisite carvings of animals and humans, as well as elaborate inscriptions. Just behind it is Sridigamber Jain Temple.

On the way back to the main shrine, we walked past a group of elderly Indian tourists sitting in line along the paved path. Something about the way they were perfectly lined up, all holding umbrellas to shield them from the sun, reminded me of a kindergarten class on a trip.

"You should learn a thing or two from them about discipline," I said to my kids, laughing. They did not find it funny.

By the time we made it back to the main shrine, it had reopened, and we were able to walk around and examine a breathtaking array of relics, frescoes, and statues.

Julian was particularly happy to have visited the complex. He had just become a student of Buddhism and everything about it fascinated and excited him. Acknowledging his enthusiasm, I asked our driver to stop in front of another Buddhist temple we saw on the road back to Varanasi. It was small but full of frescoes and paintings depicting various stages in the life of Buddha.

We were very excited to head back to Varanasi until the driver declared that we had to stop in front of yet another place.

"Where did he say we're going?" The kids had problems understanding his English.

So did I. "No idea," I said.

I knew exactly where we were the second we got out of the car. It was one of the reasons I shied away from guided tours: guided shopping. The driver pulled up in front of what looked like a typical money trap for rich Western tourists: an emporium of various local handicrafters selling overpriced goods to tourists looking to buy something—anything—to show to their friends when boasting of their travels. I hated those places, but we were already there. The shop owners, who were sitting on small stools in front of the building smoking and drinking tea, momentarily got up at the sight of our car. Judging by the greetings exchanged between them and our driver, it was clear they were old friends or at least business associates. I desperately wanted to climb back into the car and leave. Instead, I produced a huge grin and with a loud *namaste*, motioned the kids to follow the shop owners down the stairs and resigned myself to a torturous experience of tourist shopping.

As if examining dusty souvenirs was not agonizing enough, we were first led into a room where two women clad in bright red saris were chatting in front of what looked like fabric presses. At the first sight of visitors, they sat up, turned to their respective machines, and in well-rehearsed, almost robotic movements, proceeded to demonstrate how thread becomes fabric. Their demonstration was voiced over by the shop owner, who described to us every detail of this laborious and time-consuming process. We feigned interest and followed him to the next room, where this very fabric was going to be sold to us.

Determined to make the best of it, I decided to at least use this time to our advantage; my in-laws had an anniversary coming up the week of our return. A tablecloth could be a nice gift, considering how beautiful the Indian silks were. I also could buy a scarf for my mother-in-law's birthday, and the pain of travel shopping could be behind us. The kids and I were led to a large room lined with various types of fabric along all four walls. Next to one wall was an empty glass counter with a soft bench in front. We were shown to the bench. The salespeople proceeded to unroll reams upon reams of fabric on the counter in front of us: sari fabric, better sari fabric, the most beautiful sari fabric. It took me about ten minutes to finally explain to them that the only things I might be interested in were tablecloths and scarves.

Without missing a beat, salespeople switched from saris to tablecloths and scarves, unrolling them in the same fashion in front of us on the counter. We quickly chose the fabrics we liked, but it took another ten or fifteen minutes to bargain for the right price. The shop owner punched the price on a large plastic desk calculator and pushed the calculator to me. I feigned shock, cleared his number, and punched my own before pushing the calculator back to the shop owner. He expressed sadness at my number, shook his head, smacked his lips, punched another number, and pushed over to me. It went on like this until we agreed that I would pay one-quarter of the price he had originally offered. The next shop we were obliged to visit was less enticing, as we had no interest in plastic jewelry or wooden goddess statues. Exhausted by the last visit and hungry, we complimented the owners on their beautiful wares and rushed to climb back into the car to go have some lunch.

We were still on the outskirts of Varanasi in a residential area that was somewhat less crowded and congested. It took us only a few minutes to pull up in front of a restaurant located on the second floor of a new glass building. We were the first visitors to the restaurant. Our appearance excited the staff and we were shown inside to choose a table. It was a truly tough choice, as the restaurant had no air-conditioning. They did have a number of ceiling fans located sporadically throughout the restaurant. However, the fans would not be turned on until we sat down. At least the food did not disappoint. While the kids were happy chewing on goan chicken curry, I discovered delicious seekh kebabs, which are vegetarian shish kebabs ground to the consistency of meat and prepared tandoori style, not unlike their meat counterparts.

After lunch, the driver drove us back to the main square, where we made arrangements for the following day and set off to the hotel on our own. We took our time strolling through the marketplace that sold every household item anyone could ever need, from plastic buckets to propane tanks, from old furniture to plastic toys, from metal pans to cotton bras, and everything in between. We did not feel pressured by the vendors, as they knew we were not their buyer contingency and left us to leisurely wander around the market examining the goods and observing transactions.

By now we had learned to navigate the narrow alleyways leading from the main square to the *ghats*. Julian even waved to the resident bull, which was escaping the afternoon heat by reclining in the shade across the already-narrow passageway between the buildings.

We had some time before our sunset boat ride so we went past our hotel and down to the Ganges. The Ganges is the heart and soul of India. The story of the Ganges is the very story of India itself: its rises and falls, its victories and conquests, its culture and traditions. Millions of Hindus worship the Ganges. It is a goddess who liberates them from the cycle of life and death; it forgives their sins and heals their sick. Every year, hundreds of thousands of pilgrims travel long distances to deposit the ashes of their loved ones in the waters of the Ganges to facilitate their passage to heaven. At least once in his lifetime, every Hindu will bathe in its waters.

Its former and present glory notwithstanding, the first sight of the Ganges is shocking. This exalted body of water is so filthy and polluted that I could not help but feel incredibly sad at the sight of its defiled banks. My sadness was overcome only by a wave of nausea, which struck me as soon as we descended the *ghats*. No words could adequately describe the stench surrounding the Ganges. All the adoration does not stop its loyal worshippers from dumping all sorts of garbage into its waters; from food refuse to industrial waste to urban litter, everything floats in the waves of the Ganges. Hundreds of thousands of people who so lovingly pray at the banks of the Ganges do not hesitate to urinate in its waters or defecate on its shores. The smell of wet garbage mixed with human waste and various body odors was—and still is—the strongest stench I ever experienced. It was very difficult, as we walked along the river, to separate our nostrils from the Ganges experience. I think the kids may have had a harder time of it than I did, as I had come here prejudiced about the city's holy history and the river's glorious past.

Not only did the kids have trouble with the smells, but they also became very unnerved by the spectacle we created everywhere we went. My salwar kameez did not help me blend in as I had hoped it would. My longhaired kids attracted attention much like a freak show that came to a small town. Adults just gawked or pointed fingers. Little kids followed us and even tried throwing small objects, like sticks or pebbles, in our direction. Groups of teenagers gathered around us and pointed while laughing loudly and talking about us in a language we did not understand. While all this attention was making Julian uneasy, Fillip, shy and introverted by nature, was so agitated by it that at certain moments I expected him to burst out crying. He held it in.

"I hate it, Mom. Everyone is staring at me."

"They're staring at me, too." I guess I was not very consoling. "It's because these people never saw such ugliness before." My joke went absolutely flat.

Some kids tried touching Fillip, which made him jumpy and even more grumpy. I wished there was something I could do to compel him to enjoy Varanasi as much as I did. Our tensions eased with the sudden appearance of a *sadhu*, an Indian holy man. Dressed entirely in white, in stark contrast to his brightly colored face and unkempt dreadlocks, he was extremely tall and powerfully built. His graying hair betrayed his otherwise youthful appearance, and the sagging skin on his arms revealed a much older man than he seemed at first glance. We were so preoccupied with our little world (with Julian falsely trying to seem blissful, Fillip being totally miserable, and me trying to lighten everyone's mood) that we did not see him or even clearly understood where he came from. He just appeared. All three of us almost tripped over him as his large body just materialized on our way.

"Are you the hidden messiah?" the *sadhu's* voice roared as he placed his long-nailed crooked finger right in the middle of Fillip's forehead, stopping the latter dead in his tracks.

Horrified, Fillip, still unable to move, slowly rotated his head in my direction, with the *sadhu's* finger still attached to his forehead. I opened my mouth, but nothing came out.

"I don't know," murmured Fillip, staring wide-eyed at the *sadhu.*

"Hmm," growled the Sadhu, clearly unconvinced, but he let go of Fillip's forehead nonetheless.

The three of us swiftly shuffled off and it was only after we were a safe distance away that we stopped short, looked at each other, and burst out laughing uncontrollably.

"Ha-ha, hidden messiah," we could not help snickering.

"Does that make me the mother of the messiah? Are there special privileges that come with that?"

"Ha-ha, where were you hiding?"

"The next time someone asks you if you're a hidden messiah, just say yes!"

With our moods livened and the tension gone, we were able to continue enjoying Varanasi and all the sights it had to offer.

Walking along the Ganges transported me into my childhood, where, open-mouthed, I had watched documentaries about the city of Benares, its holy past, and its continued traditions. Nothing had changed from the years of those documentaries to the year of our visit. In fact, nothing had changed in that city for centuries. All along the river Ganges, life went on as it did a thousand years ago. Scores of monkeys chased each other from rooftop to rooftop. People bathed in the Ganges; some swam, some just immersed their bodies to the waist, others would cover their noses and go under. A boy of about thirteen was squatting on a staircase holding what looked like a tunic. The boy was rubbing it with a bar of soap, wetting it with some water from a metal cup (no doubt full of water just retrieved from the river), and beating the tunic on the stairs. He kept repeating the process while the man next to him, wearing nothing but underwear, was brushing his teeth with a finger of his right hand and holding tooth powder in the open palm of his left. A group of women near them were lighting tiny oil candles to be sent down the river in marigolds as a ritual offering. They stopped to pray while covering their faces with both of their hands. Periodically, one of them would cup her hands and take a drink of the Ganges water—garbage, dirt, and all.

"You know, even if I did not drink the water but just swam in it, I'm sure I would end up in the hospital," I mused out loud to the kids, who just took it all in wide-eyed.

Loud music was blasting from the speakers strategically placed in most *ghats*. Interestingly, each was playing a different tune, overlapping in some spots and creating an unruly cacophony. I laughed when in one of the speakers I recognized the famous "Hare Rama Hare Krishna" chant mixed into a modern techno-like beat.

Elongated rowboats and large mechanical barges transported people from *ghat* to *ghat*. Some carried *sadhus* who led Hindus in prayer as they took in the sights of old Benares. Some were filled to such capacity that I was sure I would witness an accident; I expected these barges to overturn or sink under such a load. Such thoughts did not seem to preoccupy the boat passengers, as some of them were standing up, holding large umbrellas and even swaying from side to side, deeply immersed in prayers.

We walked along the riverbank to what looked like a marketplace, where most of the displayed wares seemed to reflect the religious nature of this place; offering garlands, candles, and various images of deities were spread out on large blankets on the ground. Here the vendors did not seem to push their goods, but merely sat back and let the buyers come to them. It did not seem a difficult feat, as everywhere I turned, people were bargaining, arguing, paying for things, or trying things on.

As we walked, I spotted a woman squatting on a small blanket on top of the stairs. She was a leper. Although she looked a lot older, the jet-black color of her hair revealed that she was probably in her thirties or forties. Her entire body was covered by large bulbous ulcers, which caused her limbs to bend inward and her right eye to stay shut. She sat meekly next to two elongated metal containers and a small shopping bag containing something that resembled food. She did not beg or peddle; she merely looked up with her one good eye at the passersby, eliciting pity and meager donations of money or food. I am not sure which of us was more horrified: the kids when I told them about leprosy or me, a delusional Westerner who believed that leprosy had been wiped out centuries ago.

Goats were grazing on some of the concrete-covered hills between the *ghats*. I could not help but wonder what these poor animals could find to eat aside from some cigarette butts and candy wrappers. My kids stopped to photograph the goats.

"You poor deprived child," I joked with Julian, "You don't seem to have ever gone to a zoo." In reality, we just could not help ourselves.

Everything about Varanasi was striking and exciting, and goats on concrete were no exception. The three of us just kept snapping away at everything we saw.

We had about thirty minutes until we had to meet the boatman, so we went up to the hotel lobby to wait for him and get some rest after being on our feet all day. We sat on a sofa and proceeded to exchange impressions of our first two days in India. Fillip took out our small digital camera and turned it on.

"Wow, Mom, did you know we already shot over three hundred photos? And that's just in two days."

"I know, but how can we help it? Everything around us is so different and so interesting."

"Except for this one," announced Fillip, showing me a photo of himself that he disliked. "I look horrible," he proclaimed in disgust. "Can I delete this one?"

"Fine, delete it," I agreed, "but don't touch any others; we'll sort them out when we get home and filter the bad ones then."

I actually watched Fillip press the button. I am not sure what he was thinking or why I wasn't quick enough to stop him, but in just a fraction of a second, before I could even blink, he pressed the button. I gasped. Instead of the one bad photo of himself, Fillip had deleted all of our photos from the previous two days—every last one of them. For the next few minutes, Julian and I just stared at Fillip in disbelief. Fillip stared back at us in just as much disbelief, finally uttering, "I'm sorry, it was an accident."

"An accident? You just got rid of all of our photos. All of them— Humayun's tomb, Varanasi, Buddhist temples, holy men— they're all gone."

"It was not my fault. It was an accident."

"You cannot touch this camera ever again for the length of this trip. Not once. Don't even look at it!" I was mortified. "Don't even think of looking at it."

After a few more impertinent remarks from his brother, Fillip went on the offensive.

"You are being mean to me," he announced with a pout. "I think you are behaving like two jerks and I don't want to talk to you."

"We're being jerks? You're the one who got rid of all our photos. We have no photos left. Not one. We should've killed you, but no one has even yelled at you yet!"

"You're yelling now, and Julian is being mean."

This was getting us nowhere.

"All right, let's stop it. It was no one's fault. There is nothing we can do about it now, so let's just get over it. We'll take some new photos tonight and tomorrow. On our last day in New Delhi, we'll just revisit Humayun's tomb and take as many pictures there as we need. So the only thing we'll be missing are the photos from Sarnath. No big deal. We'll just have to get over it."

Still brooding over the photos, we followed our boatman from the hotel down to the river. He led us through piles of garbage and onto a small wooden rowboat. It took some skillful maneuvering on our part to avoid stepping into the mounds of debris and refuse covering the shores of the Ganges; we had to hop over trash heaps straight into the boat. Olga Korbut would be jealous.

Our boatman wore the same blue checkered shirt we saw him in earlier. It looked washed and worn, its color faded. It was, however, immaculately pressed, and it seemed oddly mismatched with the beige sweatpants he was wearing. We were in awe of him. His English vocabulary list totaled twenty words at most. But it was not a deterrent. As any good guide would, he insisted on pointing out Varanasi's landmarks. Unfortunately, neither I nor the kids could understand him. Our conversations went like this:

"Fheros sdlfueklio rueding fromeo."

"Right."

"What did he say, Mom?"

"No idea."

Never one to give up, I still insisted on asking him questions. Unfortunately, everything that sounded like a question automatically solicited a positive response with numerous confirmations.

"Have you been doing this for long?"

"Yes, yes, yes."

"Are there any fish in the river?"

"Yes, yes, yes."

"What kind?"

"Yes, yes."

"What is your name?"

"Yes, yes, yes."

Thank God for guidebooks; upon our return to the hotel, I was able to find and explain to the kids most of the landmarks we had passed. There was one spot to which the kids and I were drawn like a moth to a flame: the burning *ghats*.

There are two burning *ghats* in Varanasi: Manikarnika and Harishchandra. The larger one, Manikarnika, conducts up to two hundred cremations each day. A cremation at Manikarnika is a very business-like, efficient transaction. Huge stacks of wood are placed on the plateau above the *ghats*. The family of the deceased buys one of the many funeral packages offered as part of the service, the prices of which depend on the financial situation of a family, they would pay more or less, based on the type and quantity of wood they choose, the ghee, and the priest's services. Cremation is a male affair, as only the men of the family watch the ceremony; the women do not come down to the burning *ghats*.

Workers fetch the body and place it on the pyre. The priests chant and perform ceremonies before the ghee is poured on the pyre and is lit. It is not unusual for the family to not be able to afford enough wood. In those cases, a body is burned in phases. The mid-section is burned first, followed by the head and legs, which get pushed into the pile by a long pole. The eldest son or a senior male of the family then gathers the ashes and unburned bones and scatters them into the holy waters of the Ganges, with the hope that the sacred river will help the deceased reach heaven.

All along the burning *ghats* are a number of men with nets who sift through mud and ash hoping to find jewelry that may have been left on the deceased. I was later told these men are from the "untouchables" caste. Not everybody is cremated; *sadhus*, pregnant women, children under five, lepers, snake-bite victims, and animals are thrown into the water with a weight tied around their necks. Unfortunately, the weight is often not sufficient, and it is not unusual to see a body floating in the waves as one takes a scenic trip down the river. Thankfully, the only body we saw floating was that of a cow.

Our boatman asked us not to take photographs or film the cremation ceremony, so we floated by them in silence. It was only when we started to tear from the smoke blowing into our eyes that I realized how close to this scene we really were—not just physically, but spiritually. We may live thousands of miles away, we may dress and speak differently, but in the end, we will all join each other in this same cloud of dust.

With the promise to visit the other cremation *ghat* in the morning, we turned back. No more than five feet away from the burning pyres, we saw a bunch of kids swimming in the river. They were diving into the water off the nearby rocks and waved at our boat as we passed by. Next to them, an old man sat in his underwear, dangling his legs in the water. Further along, a group of women were washing clothes in the Ganges.

"Life goes on," I thought.

Deep in contemplation, I did not even realize how dark it had become, as the sun had finally gone down. Suddenly, the shores were lit up with millions of lights. Streetlights, candlelight, decorative lights—they were colorful and bright against the stark background of the city walls. Hundreds of thousands of people were pouring onto the shores of the river in preparation for a festival. By now I knew better than to ask our boatman about the celebration. There were people singing into loudspeakers, priests reciting prayers, and people swaying in unison. A feeling of happiness and celebration was in the air, and we could not help but feel some of it spill over into our boat. Our boat reached a floating 'offering kiosk' where we purchased three lotus flowers with tiny oil lamps and sent them down the Ganges in an offering to the gods.

We were still in this state of euphoria when we went up to the rooftop restaurant of our hotel to have dinner. The air was oppressively hot and humid. Combined with the stench arising from the river, an outside meal was probably not the best idea. But for the next two hours, the kids and I sat on top of the river, watched the festival, and discussed our impressions of the holiest Hindu city. My only concern that night was the fact that Fillip, introverted as he was, still could not get over being a center of attention for the locals. He loathed what he perceived as people making fun of him, and it made him uneasy. I could not lie to him and tell him it would change. The best I could offer was suggesting that eventually he would get used to it (oh well, I never claimed to be in possession of "the most capable parent" prize).

That night I did not sleep. The kids were exhausted and were out like a light. I, on the other hand, spent a night listening to our room air conditioning. The unit was a huge rusty behemoth that kept shutting off every twenty minutes, loudly announcing the imminent shut-off each time. It would start with a shake followed by a loud bang that would turn into a low grumble before total silence. Then, with a hiss and a few shakes, the unit would start working again.

At four thirty in the morning, our alarm rang. We were meeting our boatman at the hotel at five o'clock. Hoping for a better shower at our next destination, I settled for some cold water on my face and bottled water to accompany the toothpaste on my toothbrush. The kids did the same, and by five o'clock we were walking along the path to the docks.

Although the sun was not even visible yet, crowds of people already were gathered along the shores of the Ganges. Some were bathing, others were brushing their teeth with river water, and still others were chanting or sending flower offerings down the river. People carried the towels down to the river as we would into a shower.

"Did you apply mosquito repellent?" I don't know why I worried about that at the moment, and the concern seemed so random and frivolous to the kids that they burst out laughing.

"Mom, it's not even six o'clock. We are sailing down the Ganges while people are swimming in the same water where bodies are floating, and you're worried about mosquito repellent?"

They were right; everything other than the spiritual seemed frivolous and mundane on the Ganges.

A little after six o'clock, we saw a red disk appear on the horizon across the river. It grew steadily and the sky started to assume shades of gold. Just then I spotted two boys of about twelve rowing a wooden boat. To this day, when I think of Varanasi, this is the image my brain conjures up: two tiny silhouettes against a huge red sun disk, the rising star of India.

It was not yet seven o'clock when we docked our boat and, hopping over heaps of trash, followed our boatman up the stairs away from the river. Just when I thought we were on our way to the hotel, he motioned us to follow him into one of the tiny streets of the city walls. He accompanied his gestures with explanations, but they were lost on us. Before any of us realized where we were, we found ourselves in a large room lined with fabric from floor to ceiling. Promptly, a young man came in, greeted our driver (who said his good-byes then), and motioned us to sit on a rug. Just like we had seen a day earlier, he proceeded to unroll reams upon reams of fabric in front of us, accompanying each ream with a full detailed description of its virtues. The kids and I resigned ourselves to more torturous fabric shopping and it was not until I finally agreed to purchase a tablecloth for myself that we were able to leave the shop. Four years later, the tablecloth is still in my closet, unused.

After a quick lunch at the hotel restaurant, we said good-bye to Varanasi. There was something about that city that resonated with me. Perhaps one needs to see more of the world to appreciate it; perhaps one needs to experience more. Whatever it is, it is a city that that took up permanent residence in a corner of my heart.

Varanasi airport defies description. It is a large, messy room that reminded me more of a waiting room at the DMV than an airport. Perhaps it was the weather or the time of year, but the airport staff easily outnumbered the passengers. There were groups of two or three people scattered around the main lounge, which was nearly deserted. It took us a number of tries to find our terminal as the signs were less than direct, and each airport employee we approached pointed us in a different direction. After about forty minutes of wondering, we finally found ourselves at the terminal surrounded by a crowd of about sixty people.

So this is where everyone is, I thought, leading the kids to the only empty row in the back of the terminal. We situated ourselves on extremely uncomfortable black faux-leather seats, took out our books, and got settled in to wait for our flight. We were deep in our books when a boarding announcement was made for a Mumbai flight. As if by pulled up by an invisible string, the whole terminal rose as one huge mass and proceeded to the gate. Within minutes, there were only five people at the terminal: the three of us and a couple from the Netherlands, a husband and wife who were both over six feet tall decked out in the latest European couture.

We had never flown Kingfisher Airlines before, but no matter how bad the flight could be, it was only forty-five minutes from Varanasi to Khajuraho, so we chanced it. The experience was so different from our expectations. To begin with, we had a 737 plane almost all to ourselves. The only other passengers on the flight were the couple from the Netherlands who sat two rows behind us. The plane cabin looked new and clean, which seemed like a great feat to us, having just left Varanasi. The crew, either out of boredom or perfect training, anticipated and serviced our every request. They kept bringing toys and crayons, which sent the boys into hysteria, as they thought them-selves too old for such activities. At certain moments, I even found myself wishing the flight would last longer, as I was finally enjoying the small creature comforts, like hot water in the lavatory, that I had been missing for the last three days. But all good things must come to an end, and we pulled up to a terminal gate in Khajuraho right on schedule.

Chapter 5

KHAJURAHO

The airport in Khajuraho was extraordinarily tiny, and it was a true wonder how a big plane like ours landed there. For the moment, however, we were not concerned with the minutia of modern aviation; we were busy collecting our luggage and figuring out where we would reunite with Kamal. We walked down a dark terminal corridor into the bright light of an April midday sun. I looked around. There was a parking lot right across the street from the airport exit. Three cars were parked in the lot; none looked like our bony Land Cruiser.

"Do you see him, Mom?"

"No, but why don't we just stop here so that when Kamal arrives, he can spot us easily." Not that it was difficult to spot us; the Dutch couple had already left with their driver and we were the only people standing on the walkway between the terminal and the parking lot.

As I was looking out into the distance, I did not even notice a short heavyset man, dressed in all gray, sprinting toward us. But suddenly there he was, right next to us, wearing the biggest grin I have ever seen anyone produce. He was holding up a familiar cardboard sign with the name "Magolez" written on it.

"Madame, Madame." The short distance he ran had knocked the wind right out of his stubby body. "*Namaste*, Madame. I am Sanjay."

"Sanjay? What happened to Kamal? He was supposed to meet us here—"

"Yes, Madame. Kamal had car trouble, so boss asked me to come. I am Sanjay."

"Nice to meet you, Sanjay. The kids and I shook hands in introductions. "Will you be with us for the next two weeks?"

"Yes, Madame. I will drive you."

For the next two weeks, the kids and I got to know Sanjay very well. He was one of those people it was impossible not to like. Sanjay was a dark-skinned man in his forties. He stood about five feet, six inches tall and sported a perfectly round belly and a permanent smile. At times, when he thought a smile was not required (as in a photograph), he would produce what he thought was a serious face, but looked more like a caricature of a stern demeanor. Sanjay hailed from Kashmir, where his wife and ten-year-old son lived near his brother, who ran the family farm.

Sanjay worked as a driver nine months out of the year, going home only for the Indian monsoon season: May to August. That's when jobs were almost nonexistent as the tourist seasons wound down. He called home a few times a week from a cell phone issued him by his boss. He missed his family and spoke of them often and fondly. Everything Sanjay earned was sent back to his family to pay for his son's education and to help the upkeep of the farm. Although there are government-sponsored schools in India, Sanjay informed us that anyone with any money did everything possible to send his child to a private academy. There, unlike in public schools, children generally were assured of air-conditioning in the summer and heat in the winter, running water, and teachers who showed up for class. But all good things come at a cost, and in addition to tuition, parents had to pay for textbooks, uniforms, and other school supplies.

Sanjay's wife, who was his distant cousin, did not work but helped out on the family farm, in addition to raising her son and keeping the house. She had one request of Sanjay: she wanted a camera—a simple point-and-shoot camera. Sanjay had a big family back home and there were always celebrations—weddings, birthdays, etc. Sanjay's wife wanted to capture all those precious moments. Therefore, Sanjay was saving money for a small camera. During the two weeks we spent together, I would tell him everything I knew about cameras and he would diligently do his price research. Every few days, he would inform us with a big sigh that the prices were still too high, so the camera purchase was not yet on the horizon.

Upon meeting Sanjay, we were happy to learn that he spoke English. Even if there were times we had to ask him to repeat something so we could understand, and even if there were times that numerous repetitions didn't help us understand, his English was good enough for us to chat it up for two weeks. Both the kids and I would teach Sanjay new English words. He, in turn, taught us basic Hindi.

Sanjay's car, on the other hand, left us pining for Kamal's Land Cruiser. It was an old Hindustan Ambassador. I have only seen cars like that in old Hollywood films of the 1960s. It was a bulky white machine that would fit right in on a farm in Oklahoma, circa 1959. Its seats were worn-out leather imitations. To keep them somewhat presentable and to keep the heat off the leather-like fabric, Sanjay kept towels on all of the seats. The towels were not big, and we learned to move them strategically so we wouldn't have to keep fixing them for hours on a road. There was nothing automatic about the car, which included windows that took some strength to open or close. The clutch looked like it grew out of the car floor where it ripped an ugly hole through the linoleum. Every time Sanjay changed gears, the stick continued to vibrate long after being touched. There were times I worried it would finally be ripped out of its hole one day, but it persevered. And after Sanjay assured me that the prime minister of India himself prefers to drive in the Ambassador, I could not help but be impressed by this four-cylinder anomaly of the automotive industry.

"I will drive you to hotel, Madame," announced Sanjay. "How long do you want before I come back to take you to temples?"

"Will it be too late if you came back for us at five-thirty?"

"Not at all, Madame. It will be not so hot then and temples open late anyway."

The Taj Chandela hotel in Khajuraho was a pleasant surprise of peace and tranquility. Coming from Varanasi, we were thrilled to find the hotel in the middle of what looked to be a very quiet village center. It seemed worlds away from the crowds, noise, and dust of Varanasi. On the contrary, the hotel was surrounded by a serene, well-kept garden. I was still checking in at the reception desk when the kids informed me that there was a giant pool at the hotel that was calling our name.

"I'll tell you what: as soon as we drop off our luggage, we can go for a quick dip before heading out to the temples."

Our room was on the first floor with a patio door leading to an almost-homey backyard. In the ten minutes it took me to clothe myself and put away our things, the kids were already outside playing with a beach ball they found next to the room. The three of us headed for the pool, and the kids made a mad dash and dove in with a loud splash. The most reserved of the trio, even I found a dip in the pool refreshing, despite the fact that the water contained enough chlorine to kill every germ known to man. The kids were even happier to find a Ping-Pong table right next to the pool. They spent the next hour swimming and playing Ping-Pong. Their happiness was matched only by my own thrill of finding an adequate shower waiting for me back in the room. Even though the water never reached a temperature above lukewarm, at least the stall was clean and the towels did not show any visible stains.

We met Sanjay in front of the hotel entrance and set out to see the temples of Khajuraho. Our first stop was at the Jain Temple Parsvanatha. The white cone-shaped temple is a glorious example of tenth-century Indian architecture. When built, the temple was first dedicated to Adinath, the first religious saint of the Jains. In the nineteenth century, Adinath was replaced by Parsvanatha, the Jains' twenty-third saint. Jainism is an Indian religion that encourages a path of non-violence toward all living things. Most historians date Jainism between the ninth and sixth centuries BCE and believe that its pervasive philosophy may have given rise to Buddhism. Jainism has only ten to twelve million followers, which places it among the smaller world religions. However, Jain influence in India is quite significant and widespread.

Walking into the Jain Temple grounds was a far cry from the sights of Varanasi. It was so tranquil and still that we felt compelled to lower our voices even when outside. The temple itself, although not exceptionally big, was certainly breathtaking, especially as it was lit by the setting sun. Its white stone carving reflected the sun's rays, setting the whole building ablaze. Walking through the front doors of the temple, we encountered three Indian male visitors who promptly stopped in their tracks and followed us with their eyes. Fillip momentarily looked at me in exasperation. I just shrugged at him and advised to ignore the rude behavior. Not sure if Fillip took my advice or just gave up on acknowledging his frustration, but he just walked past the stares and proceeded to enjoy the sights of the temple.

Something similar occurred outside, when we walked around the building to the dark stone elephants guarding the temple. An old man in his seventies, who squatted on the temple stairs, turned his head to follow my children's every move very intently. Julian just dismissed the old man's stares outright and Fillip decided to follow his brother's example, so the day continued without incident—rather, almost without incident. As we were leaving the complex, a group of teenagers joined us on our path. Some showed off their knowledge of the English language: "Hello, Madame. You pretty." Others just pointed and discussed us among themselves in Hindi and laughed. But it was not until one of them reached out and touched Fillip on the shoulder that I finally had enough.

"Do not touch him!" I warned as I stopped and looked directly at the offender. "Do not touch him again." I must have had a menacing look on my face, as the teenagers stopped. Sanjay, who witnessed the scene from the car, came over and walked with us.

"Do not let them touch boy," he advised. "These young men not good."

"Thank you, Sanjay, I know," I sighed.

Getting out of the car in front of the Khajuraho temples, we knew we were back in tourist bliss. Hordes of children and old people surrounded us, peddling all kinds of ware, from postcards to erotic statuettes. We had to weave and shove to make our way through the crowds of vendors and into the gates of the temple complex.

Once inside the gates, we found ourselves in front of three separate temple complexes, all built of the rich golden-brown sandstone of the area. We started with the western side and for the next few hours proceeded to explore the serene temple grounds. It was not long before Fillip and Julian started to whisper something to each other and giggle. After a few of these outbursts, I knew the cat was out of the bag: the temple's walls, floors, and walkways were covered with hundreds of thousands of carvings, each depicting a sexual scene.

The temples were built by the Chandela Dynasty, which traced its descent to the moon god. It is believed that the head of the original Chandela clan was a noble warrior who fought lions barehanded. But it is not history that renders these temples unique; it is their strange choice of decorations. The abundance of sexual sculpture at the temples has been a subject of much debate over the centuries, and no explanation was ever able to justify the sheer abundance of such scenery on all three temples. Some historians insist that these temples were once centers of tantric mysticism, which considers sex an important catalyst of achieving nirvana. Other historians insist that the temple art was a mere reaction to the austerity preached by the Buddha. And some believe that because these carvings and sculptures were placed on the outer walls of the temples, they were adorning the symbolic gates to godhead.

Whatever their explanations, the carvings were a big hit with my prepubescent sons. And as far as I was concerned, if it took something basic and crude like sex to guide them to appreciate unique and remarkable works of art, so be it. The end justified the means, especially as the excitement of sex wore off and we were able to just appreciate the delicate lace-like carvings of the temples.

Everything seemed tranquil and joyous at the complex, from a green parakeet that stared at us from a branch behind a chain-link fence to a chipmunk that drank from a tiny hole in a water pipe hidden along the edges of one of the temple walls. The kids followed the chipmunk all the way to the edge of the wall and hissed at me to not come near it, lest I scare the rodent.

"Where is he going to go," I mused, "over the edge? What is he, a kamikaze chipmunk?"

With that, I took a step forward. The chipmunk jumped. All three of us gasped and ran to the edge of a rather high temple wall. Ready to administer CPR, we found the chipmunk alive and well, clinging to the side of the wall. Who knew chipmunks could climb rock?

The setting sun finally forced us to leave the temples. Sanjay took us back to the hotel.

"What time should we leave tomorrow, Sanjay?" The next day we would be driving to Gwalior.

"I think early, Madame, maybe eight o'clock. It is maybe a six- or seven-hour drive."

"Six or seven? But it's only 280 kilometers." I knew that because I had looked up all of the distances we would be travelling when putting together our itinerary.

"Yes, Madame, but the roads are not good here," replied Sanjay. "This is India."

It was with a heavy heart that I realized that all my estimated driving times needed to be thrown out the window. While I was able to research distances on my computer in New York, not one website had warned me about the awful condition of India's roads. I still hoped Sanjay's worry about the roads was exaggerated.

Although it was already dark outside, it was still quite early and the kids asked to go swimming before dinner. I didn't mind. Earlier that day, when we were checking in, I had noticed a bar in the lobby next to the pool. I ordered myself a glass of wine and settled into a soft reclining chair to keep an eye on the kids and call my husband. For the next forty minutes, I sipped my wine and watched the kids dive and splash around an empty dark pool. There were hardly any guests at the hotel, and those who were there did not find an unattended dark pool enticing. The bar attracted a lot more attention. I was not successful in reaching my husband that night, as there was no cell service in the area. I tried switching spots and shifting the phone from hand to hand. It was a dead zone.

I finally gave up and the kids and I had a lovely dinner at the hotel restaurant. We actually had to ask the waiters to slow down. We were the only guests in the restaurant and the waiters were so anxious to finally serve someone that all four of them kept falling over each other's feet in their attempts to service us.

Chapter 6

ORCCHA

Shortly after leaving Khajuraho, it became perfectly clear to me that Sanjay was not exaggerating about extended driving times. By many countries' standards, the roads on which we drove would hardly be called roads; unpaved paths, dusty plains, village centers, maybe, but not roads. Although some of them contained a visible line separating traffic directions, most didn't, so drivers would estimate approximately where they should be and try hard to keep to their side. Many times, however, their estimates were off and it was only the ceaseless honking of horns, bells, moos, and *chalos* and some quick wheel turning that prevented numerous fatal accidents.

An Indian country road is certainly a colorful affair. Motorcycles and mopeds are abundant, as they are cheaper than cars. However, in India, the motorcycles carried whole families. We once counted eight people sitting sideways on one bike. Our other constant companions on the roads were colorful lorries; almost without exception, every lorry was lavishly painted. Some were adorned with abstract designs or flowers and others depicted scenes from *Mahaburata* and *Ramayana* (ancient Indian epic books). Numerous amulets, trinkets, and cardboard deities rattled, whistled, and screeched in the wind, adding to the already deafening noise of the road.

The buses in India are another cause for wonder. To begin with, none of the buses looked like they had been made in the last fifty years. Just like our old Ambassador, the buses represented a different era, perhaps sometime circa 1968. I also would venture a guess that 1968 was the last time they were cleaned or checked for mechanical problems. Every few kilometers, we encountered a broken-down bus. The exhausted driver would be standing outside, arguing loudly with a dozen well-wishing passengers who each insisted on offering automotive advice. Though I was used to crowds, having experienced rush hour in New York, I realized that the buses in India contained crowds that no subway-riding New Yorker has ever seen the likes of.

The windows and doors of the buses are open to allow limbs—and sometimes almost full bodies—to hang out from them. In addition to the bodies hanging off the bus, there were usually bodies atop the bus, packed just as tightly as their compatriots inside. It was miraculous that these people did not fall off at each bump. Their belongings, however, did not always fare as well. Every now and then we would encounter a stalled bus because someone's oranges (read: apples, bananas, chickens, potatoes) spilled off a roof of the bus onto the road. These scenes also were attended by a number of well-wishing passengers running around the sides of the bus and collecting ill-fated produce so that the bus could proceed.

Cars are a luxury to most country folk in India. No matter how small a car, it always looked like it was transporting a whole village; people sat on each other's laps and held on to the doors. Seat belts were rarely used, as it is difficult to extend a seat belt across three bodies balancing on top of each other.

Rickshaws are mostly a city transport, although occasionally we encountered them on village roads.

There is one other element that is prevalent on an Indian country road. It is what Sanjay called a "speed bump," and by that he meant livestock. Cows, goats, donkeys, and even camels and sheep could be seen crossing the roads, grazing alongside or smack in the middle of the "highway" or just taking a leisurely stroll in the midst the traffic. Unfortunately, no amount of horn can motivate a grazing cow to move off the road. We would spend many hours in India stuck behind slow-moving animals. *Ye hai India,* darling.

The road from Khajuraho was no exception. We drove through numerous market squares and main thoroughfares that Sanjay insisted were different municipalities, though they all looked like a continuous stretch of country life. Those were the places where any semblance of roads disappeared and we found ourselves driving alongside (or sometimes through) rows of tiny shops and kiosks made of tin and canvas. The passing traffic stirred up clouds of dust onto these stalls, and their owners could constantly be seen sweeping and cleaning the spaces inside. The problem was that all the trash that was swept from within these tents was swept back into the streets, where it was left to rot or blow right back into the stalls. Garbage was everywhere. We could even see it on the roads in the areas that did not seem populated.

Orchha was not originally part of our itinerary. But when I mentioned it to Sanjay, he confirmed that we could easily stop there for an afternoon on our way to Gwalior. Orchha did not disappoint. We were already in awe when its fort appeared on the horizon. Sanjay parked the car in the shade of the palace rampart, and we set out to explore. Sitting atop a mountain, the Orchha Fort made an impression on us the minute we stepped inside. It is an imposing structure overlooking the valley below. There were a few times when my heart almost jumped out of my chest as the kids climbed the rampart walls, but in general, the few glorious hours we were there were spent exploring the fort's numerous ramparts, winding staircases, cool courtyards, and elaborate frescoes. It was there that Fillip reminded us of his classmate who had made fun of him when he heard we were going to India.

"Stupid," the classmate laughed, "it's not India, it's Indianapolis."

Indianapolis had become an inside joke among the three of us. And while marveling at the fort, neither Julian nor I could resist: "Fillip, are you sure you should be here? Perhaps you misread your ticket? Should you be exploring Indianapolis?"

"What about Tennessee? Wouldn't you rather be in Tennessee?"

It was at the Orchha Fort that Fillip admitted that he would come back here one day. Still coming off the sour welcome of Varanasi, Fillip had thus far refused to admit he liked anything in India. But Julian and I knew better. Finally, Fillip cracked. "OK, OK. If I were to come back to India, I would come back here again."

"Aha! Can you repeat it into the camera so that we can capture it for posterity?"

"No."

That was fine. Julian and I both heard it. Fillip loved Orchha as much as we did.

Tired and sweaty, we walked down to the dusty road between the fort and the main town square. We asked Sanjay if he would join us for lunch; he refused. As always, Sanjay would wait for us in the car, settling for a packed lunch of a few *roti* with some *dal* he had made on a portable stove. I attempted to entice him once more, and Sanjay proudly told me he would accept my request only on our last day together. Until that last day, I never asked again. Sanjay would always drive us to our destinations and wait nearby to take us back. He spent his nights on the road in boarding houses, paying nominal fees for a bed in a room he would share with other drivers who serviced tourists like us. If he got lucky, he negotiated such a room in the same hotel where we stayed. Unfortunately, there were other times when the closest room Sanjay found was thirty minutes away. On those days, I would try to delay our departure to give Sanjay some extra time in the morning, but he would hear none of it. He did want to be a burden and would go out of his way to show us how much he enjoyed and appreciated his job.

Lunch in Orchha was a unique affair. We found a small restaurant on the second floor of a building conveniently situated close to the main square. The restaurant had two dining areas: outside and inside. We were torn between the idea of eating outside in the hot April sun or inside in the stuffy and humid room. We settled for stuffy and humid, hoping that at least we would have the benefit of shade. Within five minutes we had to start wiping ourselves, as sweat began to drip from our foreheads onto the table. Fillip and I were stunned to hear Julian order his much loved *masala chai*.

"In this heat? Have you overheated to the point of madness?"

Julian could not be swayed. He loved his *masala chai,* and a silly thing like high temperature was not going to come between him and his favorite beverage. For lunch, we have settled on some *naan, dal*, and meat curry. This was accompanied by gallons and gallons of water. The biggest satisfaction of that lunch came with our check; for all of our appetizers, entrees, desserts, and beverages, our bill came to 225 rupees—roughly $5.

Having satisfied our stomachs, we walked over to town. The main square was flanked by a large temple, whose name or purpose we could not find on the temple itself or in our guidebook. Julian called it "Temple I Don't Know." Hanging around the entrance was a division of soldiers who looked like they were either passing through or were there on leave. I initially hoped the soldiers would give us some protection from the peddlers and the gawkers; sadly, they perfected the art of gawking as soon as we approached. Instantaneously, two of them separated themselves from the rest of the crowd and, under the attentive stares of their comrades, followed us right into the temple.

I could not tell what they wanted, as I could not understand their pigeon English. Seeing that, they switched to Hindi, which I could understand even less. I did understand enough, however, to realize that protection was not what they were offering. Diverting the kids' attention with some mythical tales, I waltzed them right out of the temple. We headed into the square, which was more of a dusty space lined with small shops and souvenir peddlers. Music blasted from loudspeakers, rendering peddlers and shop owners mute to us. That was not a bad thing, as we were able to just walk around shrugging at everything offered to us. We stopped at a souvenir shop where Julian saw a bronze statuette of the Hindu elephant deity, Ganesha. At the age of twelve, Julian was ripe for mythology, whether it was Greek, Hindu, or Scandinavian. After a brief bargaining session, Ganesha was his for one-seventh of the originally asked-for price.

Chapter 7

GWALIOR

It was late afternoon when we finally arrived in Gwalior, a relatively large city in Mahdia Pradesh. It was very refreshing to finally find our hotel. Usha Kira Palace lived up to its name. From the outside, we thought we were approaching a palace, as the hotel is built to look very much like something we had just seen in Orchha. We were thrilled to locate a pool. After a day of walking up and down in the oppressive heat, a refreshing dip in the pool moved up to a number one spot on our priority ladder. We did not even unpack. We dug our hands in the luggage just far enough to find our swimming suits and off we were. The pool turned out to be less refreshing—and clean— than we had hoped, but the kids didn't seem to mind; they dove right in, ignoring the dried leaves and dead bugs swimming right next to them in the yellowing water. They refused to come out for more than two hours. I, on the other hand, was perfectly satisfied with a five-minute soak. Leaving the kids to enjoy the pool, I went up to the room to take a shower and change for dinner.

I heard my cell phone ring from the hotel hallway. It rang, then stopped, then rang again. The ringing did not stop until I finally reached the room to answer.

"Are you OK?" My husband sounded totally disturbed. "I have been trying to reach you and the kids for the last two days. Are you OK? Are the kids OK? I sent you a text!"

A text? Wow, for Tony to learn to use the text function, it truly had to be an emergency.

"We're fine. The phones did not work where we were. I tried sending an e-mail, a text, calling you, but nothing worked."

"You could not use a landline?"

"It would cost over $50."

"And? To hell with $50. You could spend $50 if it's an emergency."

"It was just for two days." I really could not justify spending that much money on a phone call, nor did I consider us to be in an emergency situation. But clearly the man was rattled, and I promised him that if we ran into a spot with no service again, I would use a landline to call him.

"How are the kids? Are they enjoying themselves?"

"We are all fine. Yes, the kids are enjoying themselves. They are running around the pool right now, doing some crazy acrobatics." I could see them from the window as I was speaking. They really were running around the pool engaged in some strange game that looked like a chase or some similar activity that only kids can understand.

I finally hung up the phone after three more promises of calling or e-mailing daily and went to enjoy what was going to be a great shower. In fact, it would be one of the best showers I would take in the next two weeks. The shower actually had everything a person needed: pressure and hot water. And the fact that it was clean only added to its merits. I did not want to leave.

I was still in the shower when the kids returned.

"Mom, you won't believe what's down there." They were out of breath and knocking each other over with excitement.

"What's down there?" I could not imagine what had caused such agitation.

"Bats!" declared the kids in unison. "Lots of bats, and we were trying to catch them."

"Why, on God's green earth, would you want to do that?" I was flabbergasted. "If I see a bat, I run away from it, not toward it."

"Yeah, but that's you."

"Boys will be boys," I thought as I chased mine into the shower. The shower had the same effect on my kids that it did on me. Each of them soaked himself under a steady stream of hot water for at least half an hour. I, in the meantime, washed our swimming suits and hung them up to dry in the bathroom foyer, hoping I wouldn't forget them in the morning.

Between the kids' showers and my own hair and makeup routine, it took us awhile to get ready and it was almost nine o'clock when we finally went to dinner. The hotel restaurant looked like something out of colonial India: marble floors, large wooden tables topped with heavily starched tablecloths and equally starched napkins, expensive silverware, and elegant carved crystal. Making the scene even more decadent (or comical, as it seemed to me) were white-gloved waiters who bowed at each request and called my children "sir."

"And what would you wish to drink, sir?"

"More bread, sir?"

"Is everything to your liking, sir?"

"Look at them," I desperately wanted to scream. "Only fifteen minutes ago, these 'sirs' were chasing bats around the pool area. And these 'sirs' are so hungry that if you cooked the very same bat and presented it to them in a curry sauce, it would also be to their liking." In the end, I did nothing to spoil the ambiance of the restaurant and indulged the illusion of a long-gone era.

The next morning, Julian woke up with a cold. I berated him for catching a cold while chasing bats at night. During my "I can't believe you have a cold while it's 45°C outside" monologue, Julian stared at me in disbelief as I rummaged through the medicine bag to find the right pill. It was only after the child took enough medicine to fight off werewolves, not just a common cold, that we finally left the room.

After a brief breakfast, we checked out of the hotel and drove to the Gwalior Fort. Situated atop a steep mountain overlooking Gwalior, the fort was the reason we wanted to see Gwalior. Built in the eighth century CE, it is one of the largest forts in India. Gwalior Fort is also famous for being the first place in the world that recorded the use of a zero. We were somewhat disappointed, however, at the sight of the fort, as it looked very run down and unkempt. The photos of the fort that enticed us to Gwalior had likely been enhanced or taken a long time ago. What we found, to be sure, was a magnificent piece of architecture that, sadly, did not look like it was given the respect it deserved. Most of the original wall paint had peeled off, and only segments of the building still showed the vibrant mosaics that once covered the whole complex. I desperately wished to write a letter to someone demanding restoration. Alas, decaying landmarks would later prove to be a leitmotif of our Indian adventure. I suppose when one thinks of the poverty in India, restoring landmarks takes a backseat.

I was still deep in thought about the merits of landmark repairs when we walked up to the entrance to the fort. As the only tourists around, we were instantly surrounded by a number of "guides." These men can be found in front of every tourist site in India. They usually speak some English and wear big badges around their necks. The badges, which are too big to be believed, are supposed to assure the visitors of the legitimacy of the guides, as they are purportedly issued by the government. Their size and overall appearance usually had the opposite effect on me. It was not always easy, however, to get rid of these men. April heat and an early hour rendered us the first visitors to the site. The guides looked at us as a hungry lion would look at a passing gazelle. It was a lot easier to take a guide than to keep saying no to all of them. I finally settled on a thin dark-skinned gentleman in his thirties whose selling point was possession of a flashlight.

"There are tunnels in fort, Madame," he informed me, "and no light. There are bats. I have light." As proof, he produced two tiny flashlights. Bats! He had said the magic word; we had a deal.

Just as I thought, most of our "guide's" guidance was useless. Judging by his stories, the only thing tourists apparently cared about were harem rooms and dancing girls. We examined every harem room in greater detail than I could ever wish for.

"Blah, blah, blah...ankle bracelets...bells... music...blah, blah, blah... sex...eunuchs... blah, blah, blah...sleep with the king."

We did explore rooms that were pitch black, however, and the kids assured me that the sounds I heard were indeed bat cries. The two tiny flashlights produced just enough light to not bump into walls, so the guide served a purpose, after all.

We were very happy to be rid of the guide when we finally went back outside of the fort and wandered off to explore the rest of the grounds. On the opposite side of the mountain was a Hindu temple complex, and we wanted to visit it before leaving Gwalior.

I was convinced it was the hottest day on our trip thus far, and I couldn't believe Julian was coughing in such heat. Then I began to wonder if the hotel in Agra had a pool, as I wanted to go for a dip when we got there.

"Oh my God!" I stopped in my tracks.

"What's wrong, Mom?"

It was the pool. I was visualizing the pool in Agra: swimming in the pool, getting ready to swim in the pool, putting on my bathing suit—but there was no bathing suit! I had remembered to pull the kids' swimming trunks off the bathroom drying bar and had made a mental note not to forget to come back for mine. But then Julian had informed me of his cold, and I never went into the bathroom to collect my bathing suit. I had two options: not swim for the next two weeks or swim in the nude. Swimming pools were the only place where we could refresh after a day of walking in the heat and dust of India, as most showers were not good enough to do the job. Therefore, not swimming throughout our stay was not an option. Swimming in the nude presented its own troubles. Normally, I would not think twice about walking into a store with a legitimate excuse for a new bathing suit, but this wasn't the case in India.

I found my hotel invoice, reached for my cell phone, and tried every number combination I could think of until I finally reached the hotel.

"Hello, this is Ms. Margulis." My voice must have sounded desperate.

"Yes, Madame."

"I just checked out of your hotel a few hours ago and believe I left my bathing suit in the room."

"Yes, Madame."

"Um, yes meaning you found it?"

"Yes, Madame." I was convinced I was speaking to a robot.

"I will come to pick it up, then."

"Yes, Madame."

I hated the thought of losing forty minutes on the way out of Gwalior but had no choice; we had to go back. Before going to the car, we made a detour at a small complex of Hindu temples occupying the mountain next to the fort. I admired the intricate stone carvings on the temple walls. The kids giggled at their sexual content.

"Mom does not want us to see these," I overheard Julian whispering to Fillip.

"Little do you know," I thought to myself as I rushed them out to go fetch my bikini.

It looked like they were expecting me when we pulled up at the hotel. The second I was spotted, the receptionist produced a package wrapped in newspaper, of all things. He handed it to me and lowered his eyes.

"It's just a bikini," I wanted to laugh, "You're not handling my lingerie, you know."

Instead I settled for a quick thank you and went back to the car.

"OK, Madame?" Sanjay was perfectly calm. He did not care if we got to Agra an hour later than planned.

"Just a second, Sanjay." Now I was paranoid. It was only after a thorough inventory of all our valuables that we finally left Gwalior.

Chapter 8

AGRA

We arrived in Agra in the early afternoon. "What do you recommend we do, Sanjay?" I asked. "I read that the Taj Mahal is best seen at sunlight or sunset."

"Madame, I agree. Sunset is very nice...very nice." I will take you to Agra Fort first, then Taj Mahal."

We left our trusted driver and went to the hotel to freshen up and have some lunch. Hotel Royale Residency did not match the splendor of its name. Quite the opposite: it was a small, rundown relic of the 1970s. There were no redeeming qualities in that hotel, from the broken elevator to the dirty bathroom and low water pressure. The only thing we wished to do when we arrived at the hotel was leave it, but because we did not have much time and the hotel was located in a residential area, we could not venture far to look for lunch. We settled for an early lunch at the hotel.

The hotel dining room made up for the lackluster accommodations, not with its décor or good food, but with its tragicomical staff. The waiters and busboys were a motley crew of very young and very old. They bickered continuously for the whole duration of our lunch; the old yelled at the young, the young waved their hands in their defense and spilled beverages, the old yelled some more, the young tried to clean the spills, only to spill sugar or salt on top of the already messy tablecloths. It all looked like a badly choreographed play of an immature theater company. The only three clients in the restaurant at the time, we were either totally ignored for long periods of time or showered with forced attention from three or more waiters at a time.

In the midst of all this frenzy, I remembered that we needed to take our weekly malaria pills. That task only added to the already comical chaos of the place. I wondered what the waiters were thinking as they watched us trying to slice, crush, and bite the wretched pills to get the correct proportions. Of course, swallowing the gargantuan tablets was no easy task, as their pasty exterior and large size rendered them virtually impossible to get down a human throat. Many hot and cold beverages accompanied our efforts, and the resulting expressions on our faces stopped the staff in their tracks. As if that weren't bad enough, poor Julian had to follow that with another pill that I insisted he take for his cold.

It was about an hour later when the three of us, well fed and medicated, went out to meet Sanjay in front of the hotel.

"Madame, I first take you to Agra Fort," announced Sanjay

"Not the Taj Mahal?" – we were getting impatient.

"No, first Agra Fort, then Taj Mahal," confirmed Sanjay, and off we went.

Located about two kilometers from the Taj Mahal, Agra Fort is the most important fort in India. It was first built in the sixteenth century and served as the seat of government for many great Mughal rulers, from Humayun to Shah Jahan. The fort displays an interesting combination of Hindu and Islamic architecture. Some of the Islamic decorations even featured forbidden images of living creatures like dragons, birds, and elephants, instead of the accepted calligraphy and abstract designs.

We found ourselves in a tourist mecca as we approached the plaza adjacent to the fort. Dozens of tourist buses were pulling in and out of the plaza, and scores of tourists with hats, umbrellas, cameras, and guidebooks scrambled to follow their guides. Peddlers weaved in and out of the crowds, offering everything from souvenirs to food and various household items. Everywhere we looked, there were beggars: the blind, the crippled, the lame, and the ascetics.

Sanjay parked the Ambassador in the middle of the central square and pointed the way to the New Delhi Gate, the most magnificent entrance to the fort that also served as a ticketing counter. All we had to do was cross the street from the center of the plaza and walk up a small path leading to the gate, but this was easier said than done. Crossing the street was an insurmountable task. To begin with, the outer perimeter of the plaza was a sort of roundabout with no lights or stop signs. It had no lanes or even a clearly defined road, for that matter. So while numerous cars, buses, and rickshaws honked and forced their way ahead, the only way for pedestrians—who were also competing for street space with cows, goats, and other forms of fauna—to cross the road was to zigzag amidst the traffic, running and stopping, running and stopping to avoid being hit by one or another form of transportation. The scene looked very much like the video game *Frogger*, except louder and more involved. For a little while, I just stood there, trying to figure out how I could possibly cross without killing or maiming one or all three of us. Finally, I found the best solution I could come up with at the moment.

"Hold my hands," I said to the shell-shocked kids. "Follow me, and whatever you do, do not let go!"

The brilliant strategy I had was to zero in on a local who seemed to be a pro and follow his or her every move. We hesitated a few seconds until I spotted someone who looked like a local and who did not seem to be fazed by the task at hand. This was an older woman with gray hair, a bright yellow and purple sari, and thick-rimmed eyeglasses. She was carrying bags in both hands and had an expression of bored determination. She was clearly a woman on a mission and a little thing like chaotic traffic was not going to stop or even slow her down from wherever she was going. As she weaved her way across the honking rickshaws and cars, we shadowed her every move; we stopped when she stopped, we sped up and slowed down when she did, and finally, to our immense relief, we found ourselves on the sidewalk. Some people climb Mount Everest, others cross the Rubicon. We were happy to just cross the Agra Fort roundabout.

We made our way to the ticket counter and paid our fees, which were four times higher for foreigners than Indian nationals. Just like in New Delhi, as soon as we bought our tickets, we had to present them to a guard standing next to the counter in order to proceed. Since we knew the drill by then, we did not slow down the process and proceeded through the enormous New Delhi Gate into the fort. It was a far cry from the peaceful silence and emptiness of Khajuraho or Gwalior, and pushing our way through the crowds of the fort proved to be an ordeal.

We finally squeezed through the narrow gates and entered the first courtyard. In the middle of the courtyard were a small fountain and a few benches where tired tourists could rest before dashing off to other sites.

"Monkeys!" Before I could react, Fillip was off. On the side of the courtyard, a baby monkey was drinking water out of a garden hose. Its mother sat nearby, keeping an eye on her offspring and eating grass she ripped out of the well-manicured lawn.

"Don't get too close," I warned Fillip. "If the mother thinks you'll hurt the baby, she'll attack."

Initially, both Julian and Fillip heeded my warning and kept a reasonable distance, despite their total fascination with the baby monkey. After awhile, however, they could not help but move closer to the object of their curiosity. Suddenly, the mother emitted a loud hiss. In a split second, Fillip jumped at least four feet up and five feet back. The mother had apparently decided Fillip was way too close to her baby. She jumped between the baby and Fillip and thrust her little hand forward as if to hit him.

The kids got the hint, and we finally left the monkeys to see the fort. Our only other animal encounter happened right after that. As we were walking through an internal gate leading into the fort, a stray dog was making his way behind us, trying to squeeze through the crowd of people. As the crowd pushed into the dog, the dug brushed by Julian, leaving the latter a little bit startled and a lot muddy. The dog, having just taken a mud bath, left an impression of his entire side on Julian's leg. Even hours later, when a good bulk of the mud had dried and crumbled off his leg, the print was still clear on his shorts and T-shirt. That incident threw me into more of a frenzy than the monkey-hissing incident had.

"We did not get rabies shots," I gasped as I watched Julian get sideswiped. "Did he lick you? Did he bite you?" I was horrified and started having visions of emergency evacuation playing out in my head.

"Mom, he just dirtied me." Julian thought I had lost it. "You can't get rabies from dirt."

"How could you get so close to him? Don't you know not to touch stray dogs?"

With a shrug, Julian did the smart thing: he walked away. I still carried on for a few more minutes, but then I, too, had thought better than to spoil our trip with something as trivial as an attack of rabies.

Luckily, it was not too crowded inside the fort and we were able to enjoy it at our leisure, exploring its numerous halls and corridors. Made almost entirely of red stone, the fort was a magnificent sampling of intricate carvings and interesting designs. Almost all of its numerous high arches leading from hall to hall were covered with lace-like reliefs that still looked majestic and imposing five hundred years after being built.

Walking through the fort, we could not help but feel its dignity, but then we came to a sign posted by the Archaeological Survey of India: "Thank You for Not Scratching on the Monument."

"There goes dignity," I thought, laughing. The kids were in stitches, taking photos and recordings of the sign from every angle. In the weeks to come, we would see many similar signs; their novelty never wore off.

Suddenly, as I was still chuckling at the sign, Fillip erupted: "Taj Mahal. It's the Taj Mahal!" He made a beeline for the rampart wall, beyond which, in all its glory, stood the Taj Mahal. Julian promptly followed. The Taj Mahal had us at its first sight. Unfair as it may seem, the rest of the visit to the fort became a mere prelude to the main event.

Unfortunately, in order to get there, we were once again faced with the horrifying necessity of crossing the street. I decided to follow the previously tested method of shadowing locals. I grabbed the kids and followed a middle-aged man into the chaos of traffic. We found Sanjay with his Ambassador and took off for the Taj Mahal.

To be honest, the Taj Mahal was not the draw that lured us to India. In our travels, the kids and I generally preferred to go off the beaten path and explore out-of-the-way places that are not typical tourist destinations. We shy away from capitals and hate the herds of tourists swarming around famous sites and landmarks. However, the Taj Mahal was one of the Seven Wonders of the World, and we were not about to exclude it from our itinerary. We would go to see it, but reluctantly and briefly. Therefore, we were very surprised that at the first sight of the monument, we felt an urgent need to drop everything to go see it.

Sanjay dropped us off at the entrance to the Taj Mahal complex and explained where he would wait for us. Because of the busy roundabouts and the number of tourists around the complex, he could not wait for us where he dropped us off. So to the best of his abilities, he tried to describe our rendezvous point, while all we wanted to do was jump out of the car and go.

"Mom, do you know where we're meeting him?" asked Fillip when we were finally outside.

"Approximately," I answered absentmindedly

"Approximately? Nice. Should we be worried?" Julian was ready to start worrying.

"No, we'll figure it out later," I said, praying I was right.

The path through the park leading to the Taj Mahal was littered with peddlers and beggars. I think for every tourist in the park, there were at least four vendors trying to convince him or her to buy a deck of Taj Mahal playing cards or a fan with an image of Gandhi. And for each of those vendors, there were at least five beggars beseeching us to open our hearts and our wallets.

"*Nahim*!" I tried waving them away with a newly learned word, courtesy of Sanjay. "*Nahim*! No!"

"*Nahim?*" Most of the vendors looked quite surprised at our lack of imagination. How could I not need a Gandhi fan? We ended up almost racing to the entrance in our efforts to shake off our newly acquired entourage.

The line to the entrance was enormous. No, it was longer than that; it seemed never ending. Furthermore, it was hardly a line. It looked more like an unruly mob of people trying hard to squeeze five people at a time through the gate that allowed only one. A guard saw us walking to the line and pointed us in the direction of a small wooden shack that housed the cashier and involved another line. That line was not as bad. We purchased our tickets and quickly made our way back to the first line, resigned to spend at least an hour waiting to walk through the entry. We spent all of two minutes on that line until another guard spotted us and pulled us out of the line.

"No, Madame, there," he said, motioning us to another spot. It was also a line to the entry, but this one was a mere fraction of its neighbor. It was a line for foreign nationals. Inequality never made anyone as happy as it made us that day. As sympathetic as we were to the plight of the average Indian, we were happy to not share it at that moment. Our line contained only a few Scots, two Germans, and a gentleman from the Emirates followed by four of his wives. All four were clad in black and smelled like an airport perfume shop. Life was good.

Before we knew it, we passed metal detectors and were in front of the great gate— *Darwaza-i rauza*—the gateway to the Taj Mahal. The gate itself is a rather imposing redbrick building topped by four white cupolas. While the kids were literally squeaking with excitement, I was quickly disappointed to find out that we could not use video cameras on the grounds of the Taj Mahal. After filming a few shots from the gate (and risking the wrath of the guard at the desk), we finally set off on the narrow path leading to the Taj.

The Taj Mahal is probably one of the most recognizable monuments in the world. Built in the seventeenth century, it is a mausoleum housing the remains of the Mughal Emperor Shah Jahan and his third wife, Mumtaz Mahal. It is breathtakingly beautiful buildings and is truly a symbol of eternal love. It would be silly to start describing a building that most of us have known since childhood. We all have an image of the monument imprinted deep in our minds. So what was it about this building that enthralled and utterly shocked us, enticing us to come close? To this day, I am not sure why the Taj Mahal had such an effect on us. We were like moths drawn to a flame. We cherished every step we took along the concrete path leading through the garden and the fountains to the tomb itself. Just as we had expected, there were thousands of people strolling, praying, and wandering through the monument grounds. It did not make a difference. We slowly made our way to the tomb itself, which was becoming larger and more magnificent with every step we took.

We dutifully deposited our shoes at the bottom of the steps leading to the mausoleum and followed the crowds inside. The two lonely tombs of Shah Jahan and Mumtaz Mahal were beautifully carved and strategically placed. To us, however, it was almost an anticlimactic distraction. The outside of the Taj Mahal, its white marble walls delicately carved with calligraphy extending from the ground to the top of the minarets, held us in its spell for hours. We found ourselves wandering aimlessly, examining every curve, every stone, and every carving.

As we were admiring the tomb, some tourists were admiring us. I caught a group of teenagers trying to snap our photo from a distance, which was quite rude, I thought. I turned and covered my face with my hand. The kids followed suit. We repeated this move a few other times as various people apparently found us to be almost as fascinating as the tomb. It would have bothered us more if we had not been as elated by our experience as we were.

We were sitting on the walls of the mausoleum when a group of elderly Indians passed by us. A woman in her sixties separated from the group and made her way over to Fillip. My son became tense. She held a camera in her hands and I expected her to start snapping. Instead, she patted his check and pointed to his hair as to admire it. Fillip sat still. The woman then motioned to her camera as if asking permission to take a photo. I turned to Fillip with a quizzical look. He shrugged his shoulders; since she had asked permission, he'd allow it.

What followed was a full-blown photo session. The woman took photos of Fillip, of Fillip with Julian, of all three of us, of herself with

Fillip, herself with Julian and Fillip, and so on. During all this activity, the woman's friends stood next to us, discussing something loudly. We thought we were the objects of their conversation. Judging by their gestures and pointed fingers, I believe we probably were. They eventually left and we remained seated on the wall of the tomb. We would have sat there longer if a disrespectful eagle had not decided to relieve himself from atop one of the columns. With a huge splash, the insolent bird's excrement landed on the wall next to Fillip. Fillip was hit with the shrapnel. With a loud "Yak!" the three of us jumped off the wall and walked around the tomb to the west side of the complex, where we positioned ourselves on the floor against the outlying wall of the tomb's courtyard.

By then, we had seen every nook and cranny of the Taj Mahal complex but could not pry ourselves away from it. We watched the sun go down behind the mosque and heard the muezzin calling the faithful to prayer from its minarets. I am not sure why I assumed that just like the Eiffel Tower or the Parthenon, lights would eventually illuminate the Taj Mahal. We sat waiting for the lights until we noticed how dark it had become. It finally occurred to me that there would be no illumination. There was nothing around the Taj Mahal but darkness, which was getting more sinister by the minute. "I think we need to get going," I announced as calmly as I could.

"What about the lights, Mom?"

"I don't think there will be any, so let's leave."

Almost as soon as we walked back through the great gate, we were barraged by an army of peddlers and beggars. In the darkness, we could not tell who was who, so we just sped up our step and walked through them as if through a beehive, waving our arms in front of us and repeating *"nahim, nahim."*

"Mom, where do we meet Sanjay?" Only when the kids asked the question did I remember that I had no clue, especially in the dark.

"We'll figure it out when we get to the exit," I assured them, hoping it was true.

"Madame, Madame!"

"Thank you, God," I thought, as I heard a familiar voice. I strained my eyes to see in the darkness, but the voice unmistakably belonged to Sanjay. Apparently, we were gone for so long that he had begun to worry and decided to start walking toward us after finding a place to park.

"Are you all right, Madame?"

I am not sure which one of us was happier to see the other.

"Yes, Sanjay, we are fine. It's just that we liked it so much, it took us a long time to leave."

"I understand, Madame," Sanjay said, beaming. "It is truly most beautiful."

"That it is, Sanjay," I agreed. "That it is."

That evening, Sanjay drove us to a restaurant he claimed was "very delicious" according to his previous passengers. As Agra was crowded and it was quite late, I agreed. We pulled up in front of a building that could've passed for an ordinary diner in the suburbs of Ohio. An unassuming building, it assumed great airs once were stepped through its doors. The staff balanced turbans on their heads and maneuvered around the tables with an exaggerated sense of self-importance. The maître d' wore a thick jet-black mustache fashioned after one of the Mario brothers and hissed his esses: "Yes-s-s, Madame," "C-C-Certainly, Madame." Two middle-aged men sat leaning against a far wall of the restaurant. One of them was playing a sitar, a traditional Indian string instrument that looks like a hybrid between a guitar and a banjo. He also sang. I do use the term "sang" loosely; his high-pitched voice resembled that a tortured cat. The other musician laconically beat on the *tabla,* a pair of Indian drums. He was swaying from side to side and looked like he was about to fall asleep.

Unfortunately for us, the singing continued the entire time we were in the restaurant. To make matters worse, the restaurant did not serve alcohol. Therefore, I had to endure the entertainment in a totally sober state. The icing on the cake was our fellow diner, who sat alone at a table about five feet away from us. He arrived about ten minutes after us, and as soon as he sat down, he took out a pack of cheap local cigarettes, leaned back in his chair, and lit up. This was the only time he used his lighter. I assumed his desire to conserve lighter fluid was what prompted him to light each new cigarette with the one he already was smoking. Even as he ate, a lit cigarette rested in an ashtray next to him. He proved himself to be quite the multi-tasker when he maneuvered the cigarette in one hand while scooping *dal* in a *roti* with the other. After awhile, Julian started to cough. A bit later, I myself started to feel a rotten sensation in my throat; it became dry and itchy, and swallowing became a chore. We decided we had had enough socializing for one day, so we got the check and left the restaurant somewhat abruptly, walking out to the sounds of a rat in heat.

Chapter 9

FATEHPUR SIKRI

Fatehpur Sikri was first built in the 1570s by Mughal Emperor Akbar. Today it is a tourist attraction, an abandoned palace city situated on a rocky three-kilometer ridge, surrounded by an eleven-kilometer wall on three sides and a lake on the fourth. We had not heard of Fatehpur Sikri until the morning of our departure from Agra.

"Madame, everything all right? You have passports, cameras, and valuables?" Ever since the bathing suit incident in Gwalior, reminding me to check all belongings became Sanjay's daily morning routine.

"Um, let me check," I said. Like Sanjay, I had become more conscientious about checking my belongings before we left; once we got in the car, it would take me ten minutes each morning to ensure I had everything.

"All right, Sanjay, I have everything. Let's go to Jaipur."

"Good, Madame, but first, I will take you to Fatehpur Sikri."

"Where, Sanjay?"

"Fatehpur Sikri," he repeated triumphantly, and off we went.

The guidebook was safely tucked away together with our luggage in the trunk of the Ambassador. We would have to find out about Fatehpur Sikri as we arrived there.

After about an hour's drive we arrived in front of what looked like picnic grounds, which was as far as Sanjay could go. We would have to take a bus up the mountain. Sanjay pointed us in the direction of where the bus would be. "But the mosque there, Madame, I do not recommend," he announced to my surprise.

"Why not, Sanjay?"

"People there not good," he answered, shaking his head in disapproval.

"Well, that's silly," I said to myself. "If it's worth seeing, we'll go see it."

The grounds looked abandoned, but we trusted that Sanjay knew what he was talking about so off we went in the direction he had suggested. We walked through a number of small artisan shops on the way to the bus stop. It was still early morning; the midday heat, along with groups of tourists, had not yet reached Fatehpur Sikri. The shops seemed abandoned and quiet.

"I would like to browse the shops on the way back from the site," I informed the kids.

"That's fine, Mom, as long as it is on the way back." I bet they were hoping I would be too exhausted to even remember.

Some vendors tried to hawk their wares to us as we ascended the path to the bus stop. They were easily brushed off, however, with one simple *nahim*. The peddlers at the bus stop, however, were more persistent.

"Madame, nice necklace for you."

"No, thank you."

"But look how pretty the necklace."

"No, thank you."

"Only fifty rupees."

"No, thank you."

We were already sitting on the bus, but the peddler was intent on making a deal. "I'll make trade," he persisted through an open bus window. "I'll give Madame necklace, Madame give me watch." He pointed to a brand new watch I had bought right before our trip. It was a leather strap watch with dual time zones.

"You would have to give me many necklaces for that," I said, laughing as the bus pulled away. The peddler started to follow the bus but finally relented.

The grounds of Fatehpur Sikri were empty, with the exception of a few Indian tourists with their children and a group of Australian high school rugby players. The rugby boys were dressed as if they had just stepped out of an elite boarding school, in their neatly pressed maroon and yellow uniforms of shorts and polos. Their loud presence disturbed the otherwise sleepy atmosphere of this abandoned city. Unfortunately, we saw them at every corner we turned, and we certainly heard them well before.

After awhile, they became part of the landscape, and we spent a lovely morning climbing up and down the dusty walls of the city remains. At one point, we even followed the rugby players after we heard them clapping and yelling something. We followed the noise to the source of their agitation: a local kid of about twelve who had climbed up one of the walls in an apparent effort to jump into a pool below. We looked over the wall to see him. The kid, egged on by the crowd, was not about to relinquish all this attention in a blink. First, he carefully balanced himself on the thin wall until the expected gasps of apprehension were heard. To earn a second round of gasps, he leaned over the forty- or fifty-foot platform to look at the water below. As he pretended to become unsteady, the gasps turned into applause. It was only then that he took a few steps and jumped in. I looked down. The water in the reservoir below was Astroturf green. It reminded me of the science fiction movies I had watched as a kid in which nuclear waste always had the obligatory color of neon green. The Aussies turned wild with excitement while the kids and I walked away discussing a list of diseases we knew we would acquire if we as much as stood near that water.

We walked through the city until we finally came to the walls of the mosque. Jama Masjid, as the mosque is called, is an imposing structure with a huge courtyard. As we approached the outer walls leading to the courtyard, the muezzin's voice rang out. Groups of men started to gather in the courtyard on their way to an afternoon prayer. We were on our way to the mosque when I heard Sanjay's voice in the back of my head: "The mosque, Madame, I do not recommend. People there not good." I hesitated.

"You know what?" I said, turning to the kids. "I don't think we should go there. It's prayer time, and we probably won't be able to get in. So what do you think if we just left now?" I didn't want to alarm them with Sanjay's warnings, and thankfully, my kids agreed we should leave. We turned back to the exit gate.

"Autobus will arrive in ten minutes," the guard at the bus stop informed us. "You can wait here."

I looked around, as I was not sure where "here" was. There were no benches and worse, no shade. It was now late morning and the sun was becoming brutal. For the next thirty minutes or so, we leaned against the hot brick wall of the city gate, drinking water and counting the seconds until the bus arrived. By the time it did, all three of us looked as if we had taken a shower while wearing our clothes. Luckily, the few Indian passengers on the bus with us were just as wet and exhausted. Needless to say, it was not a pleasantly scented ride back to the picnic grounds.

As we walked back to the parking lot, I remembered that I wanted to peruse the shops. By that time, the kids had forgotten the promise made earlier and looked exasperated when I said we would make a detour. It was only after I assured them that the shopping experience would be quick that my sons followed me to the stores.

As we entered the first store, the vendor called out, "Lady, nice fabric here, very nice."

"No, thank you, I just want to look."

"But I wish to show you. Beautiful fabrics," persisted the shop owner.

I promptly left his store. After the same thing happened in two other shops, I abandoned the idea of shopping and, to the delight of my boys, informed them we were leaving.

Chapter 10

JAIPUR

The road to Jaipur turned out to be a driver's dream; not only did it get wider, but there was a clear lane separation and, in some places, even a border between the two directions of traffic. Although we were not heading drastically south, the weather started to get hotter and new "speed bumps" appeared on the roads: camels. In addition to the now-familiar donkeys, goats, and cows, we had to stop periodically to allow a herd of camels to cross the road. Additionally, wooden carts pulled by camels competed with us for traffic space on the highways.

We passed through dozens of shantytowns, where industrious proprietors set up shops along the highways. Along the highway to Jaipur, we could have bought everything we needed to prepare a meal, furnish a house, and clothe ourselves. We passed numerous tents selling mouth-watering fruit: blood-red watermelons, ripe yellow bananas, and grapes that looked as if they were about to burst from sweetness. Alas, although we would have loved to purchase some as a snack, tales of bacteria, stomach worms, and infectious diseases were lodged permanently in our heads. We would heed the warning of the traveler's health clinic we had visited before coming to India: no fruits or vegetables unless they were boiled or peeled. Indian water contains certain bacteria our Western stomachs were not accustomed to, so we would have to satisfy ourselves with produce cooked to a state at which identifying its origins became impossible.

Further along, we marveled at the number of temples "conveniently" located across the road from one another, so that no matter in which direction travelers were heading, they had no excuse not to make an offering to one of the numerous deities to whom the temples were dedicated.

While I filmed the ride and explained to Sanjay the pattern of electronics' price drops in the West, the kids played happy feet in the back seat of our Ambassador. It was a game that went on for many hours. The boys would lie down on the seat, and lean their filthy, almost totally black with dust feet on one of the car windows. The feet would acquire names, like Pablo, Fanny or Jenny, and meet, carry on conversations, form relationships and families. Thinking I was oblivious to their pastime, the boys' feet would occasionally get into totally lewd and rowdy territory. Inevitably, however, the kids would burst out laughing and move right onto a different scenario.

A few hours after leaving Fatehpur Sikhri, we started seeing signs pointing to Jaipur. Big highways gave way to smaller and sometimes unpaved roads. As I was watching the road, Sanjay made a turn and seemed to be driving away from where I thought we should be going.

"Are we going somewhere else first?" I inquired.

"Yes, Madame. Monkey Temple. Children would like it very much."

"Did you hear that, boys?" I called out to the happy feet in the backseat.

The boys perked up. By that time, their feet were happily married, had a few kids, and realized that life had become mundane. Visiting some monkeys seemed like a great idea.

To get to the temple, we had to drive up a steep wooden hill. The ascent was more difficult than it had seemed at first. Periodically, the car would hiss at us and roll back downhill. In retaliation, Sanjay would murmur something to it in Hindi, and yank on the thin clutch. The Ambassador would hiss some more, huff and puff angrily, but always relent in the end. Thus, it was with much fanfare that we drove up to the gate of the temple and almost ran over some cows amidst our arguments with the car. The grazing cows turned toward us but decided not to give way to such an ill-mannered vehicle. After a few minutes of trying to convince the stubborn animals to move, Sanjay resigned to parking the car in the shade of a tree, and we proceeded to make our way across the parking lot toward the entrance to the temple complex.

The temple was called Galwar Bagh and was built to venerate Lord Brahma, but there was something about it that was particularly appealing to monkeys. Scores of them roamed the grounds of the complex, some totally oblivious to our presence, others running after us in hopes of getting some treats. It took us some time to walk up to the gate, as the kids were thoroughly fascinated with their primate cousins. After our experience in Agra, the boys were careful not to get too close to females with babies. All the other monkeys, however, were fair game. When we did make it to the front gate, we gasped in unison; the three sides of the quadrant that made up the Monkey Temple were built into the hillside, and it was almost difficult to distinguish where the mountains ended and the temple walls began.

There were hardly any people inside the temple complex. Some local women were sitting on the walls of a building adjacent to a small Ganesha worship hall. Their curious gazes followed us intently as we took off our shoes and walked into the hall. Inside, devotional music played softly on a cassette radio in the middle of the floor. No one was there. Not knowing what to do, we walked to the end of the room and turned back to walk out. We proceeded up a hill, where a rectangular structure with carved stone arches presided over a water reservoir. In the middle of the reservoir, an elegant fountain tried hard to spit out some water into the air. Unfortunately, the best it could do was to leak some weak streams down into the reservoir.

As we walked further uphill, we were overcome by an overwhelming stench: the smell of raw sewage. It became stronger as we got closer to the water reservoir. Not unlike the one we had seen that morning in Fahtepur Sikhri, this body of water was a lovely shade of green and emanated a smell that forced us to breathe into our armpits. It was only when we walked up the steep staircase to the top of the reservoir that we noticed another, smaller body of water; it was a bath. One man was standing at the edge, drying himself with an old towel. Another man was resting on his side at the edge of the bath, an old towel covering his body. The brownish-green water of the bath, just like the water reservoir below, housed refuse: food refuse, household garbage, paper, and things we identified as dead animals. On the stone steps next to the bath, a family of gypsies was having a picnic of some *roti* and water. At the sight of us, the old woman promptly extended her hand. With her right hand extended to us, she used her left hand to point at the *rotis* and then her mouth. When she thought we did not understand, she proceeded to emulate chewing, all the while exaggerating the movement and exposing the only four teeth left in her mouth. We quietly walked away.

We would love to have spent more time at the Monkey Temple. With the exception of two German backpackers who had walked in a few minutes after us, we were the only tourists. The temple grounds were peaceful and tranquil. Unfortunately, after awhile, the smell of raw sewage emanating from the water became unbearable. Our eyes started to water and we had to leave.

On the way downhill, we passed two peacocks. The birds were flaunting their plumage, and we just had to back up to look. After taking more than twenty pictures, we finally proceeded down the mountain. At the intersection leading to the highway, we observed yet another curiosity: a boy of about eight or nine dressed in nothing but old cloth shoes and leaning against a tree stump smoking a cigarette. The kids and I cut our conversation short and stared. I was overcome by the desire to run out of the car, grab the boy, take him home, dress him, feed him, and send him to school. Sadly, there was nothing I could do.

The capital of the State of Rajasthan, Jaipur is the largest city in the state. The locals refer to it affectionately as The Pink City. Almost all of the old (and the new) city buildings are built of pink sandstone. The most famous structure in Jaipur is Hawa Mahal, or the Winds Palace. The palace is a magnificent example of Indian architecture of the eighteenth century, with its intricate latticework and nestled windows that give the whole palace the look of a huge lace beehive. Jaipur was the first planned city in India, and that fact was very apparent the minute we entered. The main roads were straight, wide, and separated by fences that were meant to prevent constant pedestrian traffic in the middle of the street. Unfortunately, these fences should have been a lot higher, as hundreds of people simply climbed right over the stubby structures and ended up right back in the middle of the road, like they were in every other town.

Entering Jaipur, we drove right into the heart of a Jain parade. Colorful floats, some of which were pulled by donkeys, were accompanied by men on horseback, elephants with painted tusks, and groups of schoolchildren in multicolored uniforms. Loud music was blasting from each of the floats, and each insisted on playing a different tune, which resulted in nothing but noise. Women, lined up on balconies along the parade route, periodically called out to the participants below and threw down flower garlands. The whole setting, while colorful and loud, was also somewhat reminiscent of our own parades in the U.S.: people marching together under various banners, accompanied by floats. As I was filming the parade, I realized it reminded me of a dance parade held annually in lower Manhattan, until I heard one of my sons shout, "Wow, he is naked. Look, Mom, he is! And there are more. They are absolutely naked!"

The second I looked up from my video camera, I knew I shouldn't have, as my eyes immediately were met with a wrinkled brown behind. The naked man was walking right next to our traffic-stalled car. My view became even worse when he turned around. There was not much to admire from the front, either. And my kids were right—there were more of them. A whole group of wrinkled old men paraded alongside our car while the kids watched in awe and

I, somewhat, in disappointment. Between Sanjay's explanation and the guidebook, I was able to gather that these men were the priests of the Jain Digambara sect, who achieved enlightenment. They shed their clothes as an unnecessary demand of the body, from which they totally detach themselves. My selfish mind wished they would attach themselves to a fitness club to make their detached bodies easier on the eyes of strangers, but I'm sure I was the only one at that parade to have such a thought.

We arrived at the hotel in the late afternoon. Everyone was tired so we made plans to meet Sanjay in the morning to see Jaipur. Stepping inside the Golden Tulip Hotel, we entered a different state and a different era. We momentarily forgot that we were in India. Very little inside the Golden Tulip Hotel reminded us that, outside, naked children smoked cigarettes and leprosy was still a threat, not unlike the common flu of the West. The hotel was modern and had every creature comfort a tourist would want. All we wanted, however, was a dip in a pool. We dropped off our luggage and went to the hotel rooftop. There was no one else at the pool, and the three of us dove right in. Surprisingly, the water was quite cold, even in the heat of the desert twilight, so after a few minutes, I got out to dry up and read while the kids continued to chase each other around the pool.

Reading quickly proved impossible as the city underneath our pool readied itself for sunset. First, a lonely star appeared in the perfectly blue sky. It was a wild scene, as the golden sun was still burning hot and the cloud of heat was still hanging low above Jaipur. Slowly, the sun turned orange, then red. With it, Jaipur was no longer the Pink City; it became scarlet red. The red sparkled against the pink stone. The streetlights, which were starting to glow all over town, also assumed a shade of red. The low hanging cloud of dust and heat started to fade and then was gone. For a few minutes, while the red disk of the sun slowly made its way below the horizon, Jaipur was ablaze. Then, suddenly, it was no longer red, but indigo as the moon took the place of the sun in the sky and hundreds of stars lit up the streets. It was so beautiful that even the kids stopped splashing and stared into the sky. Only when my body started to shake and my teeth started to chatter uncontrollably did I realize that my skin had turned blue from the cold and I needed to go inside. Reluctantly, I went back to the room while the kids stayed behind at the pool.

That evening, for the first time in days, I enjoyed a real shower. The water was actually hot and the pressure was good. I just stood under the hot stream and let the scalding hot water run down my frozen body. It was not until the kids came into the room that I relinquished the coveted spot.

The hotel restaurant was also a pleasant surprise. The décor was on par with any high-end modern eatery in New York or Paris. It was very tastefully decorated in shades of brown and silver. With the exception of a few staple Indian dishes like *dal* and *roti*, the menu was Western. I sat down at the table to order wine while the kids went to study the appetizer station, which was arranged for a buffet-style service. In a matter of seconds, Julian was back, his face beaming with excitement.

"Mom, you won't believe it," he said.

"Let me guess, they have four instead of three kinds of *dal*?"

"No, Mom, they have vegetables. Can I please have some?"

Now, I was getting excited. "Really, just vegetables? Raw vegetables?" The kids and I had not tasted any raw vegetables or fruits since we had arrived in India. Something that we took for granted back home suddenly had become a luxury that we could not allow ourselves in India.

"Really, Mom. There is salad, cucumbers, and tomatoes." Julian, who had loved salad since he was a toddler, could not believe his luck. Was I going to shatter his hopes?

"Well, OK, but just a little," I said, hoping that it was not just India but its menacing bacteria that was left outside the doors of the Golden Tulip.

That night, we had salad as our appetizer and our main course. We also knew where we wanted to have dinner the following night. The next morning, we felt like kings; not only had we had vegetables the night before, but we had a great continental breakfast at the hotel and, for the first time on our trip, we were not in a hurry, as the only thing on our agenda that day was seeing Jaipur.

We drove out of the pink streets of the city to the outskirts of Jaipur to Amber Fort. The fort is renowned for its artistic style, which combines elements of both Hindu and Mughal architecture. Construction on the Amber Fort was started in 1592 by the Raja Man Singh and continued for the next 150 years. The result is a superb majestic structure atop a mountain overlooking Maotha Lake.

We arrived at the foot of the mountain and proceeded to the ticket booth. The sun was beating down on us and the ascent to the fort seemed menacing. I suggested elephants. "Elephants? Are you crazy?" This was coming from Fillip, the same kid who had suggested we ride asses up a mountain in Santorini two years earlier.

"Why not elephants? Unlike the donkeys, elephants are steady and they do not have a habit of walking on the very edge of the path. Besides, we can all ride the same elephant, as their seats are nice and wide."

"Elephants are not in my book. No way am I riding an elephant. How could you even suggest that, Mom? Don't you see how dangerous they are?"

"Dangerous? They are as slow as can be, and unlike the donkeys that you insisted we ride in Greece, these elephants are accompanied by a handler."

"I kind of agree with Fillip," chimed in the other brave son of mine. "They do look kind of dangerous."

"What do you possibly find dangerous about them?" I gasped

"They are high, and they are fast," my ungrateful older son kept agreeing with his brother.

I looked around. The few tourists there were all ascending the slope on elephants; no one was walking. "But their seats all have shades," I said, grasping at straws. I threw one last pleading look at my not so brave but very stubborn children, and we set off for the fort on foot.

As expected, we were the only tourists on the steep path up the mountain. Along the way, we were asked to buy postcards, feed a family, and purchase a pig. The last option was presented to us in the form of a small gray piglet grazing near a mud bath along the road. The adorable swine never knew how close he came to living in New York City. The only offer we did accept on the way was a bottle of water. The heat was unbearable and the huge bottle we previously had purchased across the road was almost gone one-third of the way up the mountain.

The peddlers and beggars we encountered on the way shared their space with numerous goats that peacefully grazed along the road. The same goats, however, looked less peaceful when approached by people. Each time one of my kids came a bit too close to a goat, all I could see was the animal's horns. They horrified me. The kids, taking full advantage of my fears, did not miss an opportunity to pretend to try to tackle every goat they saw. I wished we were sitting on an elephant.

The fort itself was just as large and regal on the inside as it looked from the outside. We had fun getting ourselves lost in its numerous corridors and tunnels. After a few hours, the fort filled up with numerous tourist groups and became a bit too crowded for our liking. We left the same way we had come: on foot, down the steep slope under the scorching April sun. Elephants were still not an option.

A short drive up the mountain from the Amber Fort is the Jaigarh Fort. It was the center of artillery production for the Rajputs and is still one of the most spectacular forts in India. What impressed us most was not necessarily the fort itself but the numerous ramparts that connected the Jaigarh Fort to the Amber Fort at the foot of the mountain. The wall connecting the forts is a winding structure that sneaks through the mountains and bears an uncanny resemblance to the Great Wall of China. Wandering up and down the fort's parapets was at times unnerving, as it was a long way down to the valley below. After thoroughly canvassing the fort, we returned to the entrance gate to see its most famous claim to fame: the world's largest cannon on wheels, the Jaivana. Cast in 1720, the Jaivana is a massive structure whose front wheels measure nine feet in diameter. I laughed uncontrollably listening to Julian and Fillip engage in a discussion about the possibility of the Jaivana fitting in our living room.

"It could easily fit in our living room," declared Julian

"I think it could take a living room and a kitchen," countered his brother.

"Do you think it would fit under our ceiling? It is low."

And then: "Madame, I will be your guide."

I turned around to see an older man in a turban grinning at me as if to showcase the only three teeth in his mouth.

"A guide for what?"

"The Jaivana, Madame, the cannon." I was more amused than appalled at such audacity. I was standing in front of a huge monument marker that described the cannon in a lot more detail than I ever cared to read. Besides, the marker was written in the language I could comprehend, whereas the toothless gentleman's command of English was so crude that I could only understand less than half of what he was trying to say.

"No, thank you," I finally retorted.

"It will be cheap, Madame."

"No, thank you."

"It is not expensive, Madame."

We went at it for about six rounds until he finally fell behind when we moved away from the cannon.

At that point, it was late afternoon, and all three of us were feeling pretty hungry. We were quite ready to for lunch and headed for the exit. We were almost at the gate when I heard the boys squeal, "Monkeys!"

We had been in India for a week, and they still weren't used to seeing these animals roaming about. "Do we have to stop?" I asked. I was starving.

"Yes, Mom, just for a little while.

I sighed and sat down on a low brick fence not too far from a troop of monkeys frolicking in the shade of a large Prosopis tree. The monkeys were having a leisurely afternoon. Some were busy grooming each other. Others slept on and around the tree. Babies jumped around impatient adults, who periodically snapped at the rowdy adolescents that chased each other nearby. It was a picture-perfect moment and the kids were careful not to ruin it. They situated themselves close enough to observe the troop but far enough to not bother the animals.

"Can we go now? We have been here almost a half hour." I was hot, hungry, and tired.

"Just a little while longer, Mom."

"Now can we go? We've been here for over a half hour."

"Don't be a pain, Mom, just a little—ahh!"

Luck looked my way. While the kids were busy arguing with me, the young monkeys' rambunctious behavior finally got the best of the troop's dominant male. His patience having run out, he lashed out at one of them, baring his teeth and loudly hissing. That sent the whole monkey troop scurrying—my kids included. With a big smile on my face, I got up off the brick fence. We could finally go have lunch.

After a brief late lunch of *dal* and *roti*, we arrived at Jantar Mantar. The place is a unique collection of astronomical instruments built by Jai Singh II in the eighteenth century. It took us awhile to comprehend what we were looking at. Signs in pigeon English placed around the apparatuses only left us guessing about their purpose. Once we had it figured out, however, it turned into a rather amusing excursion as we hopped from place to place locating our astrological signs and chasing sun shadows. Once again, however, our experience was marred by a horde of tourists swarming around the complex. While half of them seemed genuinely interested in the observatory, the others busied themselves with taking photos of us.

As the sun prepared to repeat the previous night's amazing journey down the horizon, we headed back to the hotel. We drove through the wide streets of Jaipur, where the day before we had been reluctant participants in a parade. There were no signs of the night's festivities, as life had returned to normal, with people shopping, kids playing in the streets, old women observing street life from second-floor balconies, and vehicles battling pedestrians.

"From festive to the mundane," I thought as we passed through the routine chaos of life in Jaipur. Less than a month later, a series of nine synchronized bomb blasts would rock the mundane routine of Jaipur, leaving sixty-three people dead and more than two hundred injured. A Muslim militant group took responsibility, claiming to be teaching a lesson to the "Hindu infidels." By that time, we would be safely at home, watching the events unfold on TV from the comfort of our living room in New York. We would see images of bloodied rickshaws and victims with severed limbs scattered on the streets that only a week before had been brightly decorated. I would sit there with my family, fighting back tears and trying to figure out what lesson the militants thought they were teaching by taking innocent lives.

Chapter 11

BIKANER

The next morning we were off to Bikaner. Almost from the start, the landscape along the way turned into a desert—not the rocky kind, but a real yellow sand desert, sand dunes and all. Even the kids could not help but be in awe; everywhere the eye could see was nothing but sand. At some point their excitement became too much for Sanjay to handle.

"Madame, do children wish to go into desert?" he asked.

"I don't know, Sanjay."

"Yes, yes! Children wish to go into the desert," echoed my sons in unison.

Sanjay pulled over on the side of the road. The kids bolted from the car and set off running up a sand dune. A few seconds later, their speed slowed and eventually turned into a struggling climb, as the sand dune became steeper and the sun more brutal. Sanjay and I chatted next to the car while waiting for the kids to return. Every now and then, I would throw a glance at the horizon to ensure I could still see them. As long as they were within sight, I was not excessively concerned. The moment they disappeared from view, however, I panicked.

Sanjay noticed the alarmed expression on my face and tried to reassure me: "Madame, there is nothing there. Children will come back soon. Please do not worry."

Easy for him to say, I thought, working myself into a frenzy.

Luckily, within a few minutes, I was able to spot the kids' hats on top of the dune. They raced down the side of it toward the car.

"Are you crazy? Where did you disappear? I was worried sick."

"Why were you worried?" Both of them looked sincerely bewildered, "We were just looking for snakes."

"Snakes?" That is precisely why I was worried. "What snakes?"

"Sidewinders," replied Fillip calmly. "They are these deadly snakes that move sideways and leave parallel marks in the sand."

I bitterly regretted not packing any tranquilizers.

With the kids back in the safety of the Ambassador, we took off for Bikaner. It was no more than five minutes later that I noticed an ominous cloud on the horizon. From far away, it almost looked like one of the sand dunes we had just left behind. The sand dune, however, was fixed in place, while this cloud was moving rapidly in our direction.

"Sanjay," I cautiously pointed at the cloud, "is that a sandstorm?"

"Yes, Madame, but do not worry, it is not coming to us."

"Wow, how cool is that? A sandstorm, just like in the movies!" I could understand the kids' amusement but could not share their excitement. I was watching the storm intently, praying it would not reach us. The storm followed its own agenda; at first it headed straight at us, then it changed direction so swiftly that I almost breathed a sigh of relief when—"Whoa!"

For a few seconds, we could see nothing. We were surrounded by a solid wall of yellow and beige. Our car jerked and leaned to the left. For a moment, I thought it would tumble over and instinctively extended my hand to the backseat as if the weight of my arm could somehow prevent the kids from falling. And then, just as quickly as it had come, the wall receded, leaving our little Ambassador to proceed on its way.

"Wow!" The kids were ecstatic with excitement. I, on the other hand, had had enough thrills for one day. Little did I know ...

Not far from Bikaner, Sanjay made another detour. He pulled up in front of an exquisitely carved white marble temple. "It is Karni Mata Temple," he announced proudly. "Very famous temple, Madame."

"Oh, Sanjay, it's beautiful!" I exclaimed, looking at the structure in front of me. The intricate carvings on the outside of the temple were reflecting the sun's rays in such a way that it looked like the walls themselves were lit up. The sign outside read:

The 8th Wonder of the World.
Visit us at
www.karnimata.com" (sic)

Crowds of people were walking in and out of the temple. Children were playing outside, and I watched old women carry what looked like offerings of some kind into the temple.

"Madame, you can leave your shoes in the car," advised Sanjay. "It is very close to the door."

"Good idea, Sanjay," I answered, directing the kids to do the same. I regretted it almost as soon as I stepped out of the car. The paved walkway leading to the entry of the temple felt like hot coals under the burning afternoon sun. The three of us almost raced to the doors in our efforts to avoid burning our feet to a crisp. Julian, who held the video camera, ran in first. He almost bolted right out in less than a second.

"Mom! You won't believe it. This is the rat temple. The rat temple! How cool is that?"

My heart dropped. Just days before leaving for India, we had watched a program about the temple and I remember thinking that there are few things in the world less disgusting than rats, and that's coming from a Brooklyn kid who grew up sharing subway stations with the disgusting rodents. On my previous trips with the kids, there had been many instances when I was forced to overcome my fears, from donkey rides to snorkeling with urchins to jumping into icy cold water off volcano rocks. Now I had to walk into a temple inhabited by thousands of rats—barefoot!

While I was contemplating the nausea that had washed over me, the kids were already inside, so I had no choice; I stepped over the threshold to find myself surrounded by swarms of the most hideous black creatures. They were so numerous that the temple floor itself seemed to be moving. Karni Mata, a deity to whom the temple is dedicated, is worshipped as an incarnation of a goddess Durga. According to legend, Karni Mata asked the death god Yoma to reincarnate the son of a grieving storyteller. When the latter refused to help, Karni Mata promised that all male storytellers of the Charan caste would be reincarnated as rats in her temple. Only when the rats died would they once again incarnate as the members of the Depavats family, as Karni Mata's descendants are known.

The Karni Mata temple near Bikaner houses more than twenty thousand rats. These are fed by members of the extended Depavats family, who are all Karni Mata devotees. Some of these caretakers even live at the temple, serving food to the rats and sweeping rat excrement. The rats are known as "little children" and are fed grains, milk, and coconut shells from large metal bowls. Water and food leftovers from the rats are considered holy, and partaking in either is said to bring good fortune to those making the pilgrimage to the temple. Needless to say, we did none of that.

While the kids were chasing rats with their cameras, all I wanted to do was leave. Even the New York subway rats were not as oblivious to people as these rodents were. They ran everywhere: over people's bare feet, over each other, and over piles of grain their fellow rats were busy devouring. In the far corner of the temple was a large round container. It was filled with milk and its rims boasted not one, but two layer of rats; in their thirst, the rats occupied every inch of the edges of the bowl. Those that could not reach the milk climbed on their brothers' backs and drank while balancing on their hind legs, tails swinging wildly back and forth.

"All right now, we've seen the rat temple. Can we go?" I pleaded with my sons.

"I'm not done yet. I still want to see the altar on the left wall," Julian said.

"If you want, I'll leave with you." That came from Fillip. I clearly knew which son would be making it into my will.

I raced away from the temple almost as quickly as I had raced to it, with Fillip in tow. We waited for Julian back in the Ambassador.

Fillip was relaying his impressions to Sanjay. I sat in silence, still shell-shocked from the experience.

Before visiting the Fort of Bikaner, we stopped at a local restaurant for lunch. The kids, still beaming with enthusiasm, discussed the rat temple over some *dal* and *naan*. I just drank water.

Thankfully, the only other surprise that day was a good one: pulling up to the parking lot of the Junagarh Fort in Bikaner, we spotted a familiar Land Cruiser.

"Look who's here, Mom," exclaimed Julian, pointing to the car. "Kamal!"

Running into Kamal in such a random and remote corner of India was a pleasant surprise. Kamal, who was waiting for clients outside the fort, happily chatted with us for awhile. He gave us a long tale of car troubles that had resulted in Sanjay being dispatched to Khajuraho. After about ten minutes, I knew more about carburetors than I ever cared to ask.

Having said good-bye to Kamal, we spent the next hour or two wandering around the corridors of the old Junagarh Fort. With the exception of a few local tourists, the fort was mostly empty, giving us plenty of room to stroll through various harem and throne rooms, marveling at the splendor and wealth of this country's bygone era. And then, in the middle of it all, there was this sign:

PLEASE DO NOT TOUCH BASILICUM
AND DON'T SNIFF

The only way the translation would make sense is if "basilicum" was basil. Considering, however, that the sign was resting against one of the numerous thrones of the fort, we left quite bewildered. We were still laughing about it in the car on the way to our hotel.

The Laxmi Niwas Palace Hotel had been constructed as a palace for the Maharaja Ganga Singhi in the early 1900s. It is a grandiose citadel built of red sandstone. It still retains all the pretentiousness of an era long gone, and guests are treated like royalty the minute they step through the main gates.

"May I offer you some tea, Madame, while you wait for your room?" The concierge wore a huge turban and white gloves.

"That would be nice, thank you."

The kids and I dropped into comically tall wooden chairs that, despite their size, were awfully uncomfortable. We looked around the place. It almost had a feel of an old English country club that lacked subtlety and humility. There was no minimalism at this place; every corner was adorned with something. There were vases, chairs, stools, statues, benches, and so on. Worst of all were the walls of the lobby, as almost every square inch was occupied by the skin or head of some dead animal. It was almost like being in the middle of some macabre parody of a *National Geographic* special on the fauna of the Indian Desert. Gazelle heads were hanging next to full tiger skins, which were next to water buffalos and wildebeests. It was a very strange and gruesome exhibition that had quite a nauseating effect on me, the non-meat eater.

Our room was on the first floor of the palace and was just as regal and palatial as the rest of the building. Inside, however, the room looked rather empty. There were no unnecessary pieces of furniture. The enormous size of the wooden doors made it difficult for us to open and close them, and the door lock consisted of a huge padlock and an old-fashioned eight-inch key. We did our best to minimize our comings and goings.

Our only night in Bikaner fell on April 19, which was also the first night of Passover: the First Seder (Passover dinner). Our family was never known to be religious, but there are certain traditions that we keep, and the Passover Seder is one of them. This was going to be a special Passover Seder, as none of the things we were supposed to eat were readily available to us, but little details like that were not going to stop us. Back in the hotel room, I unpacked nice clothes for all three of us so that we could have our holiday. The kids asked permission to go explore the hotel grounds. Knowing how long it would take me to get ready, I happily sent my little Marco Polos out of the room, but not until after a five-minute drill on locking and unlocking our front door's padlock.

Two hours later, after all three of us were freshly showered and properly dressed, we finally left the room. Before going to dinner, we stopped at a small hotel shop that I had spotted when we first arrived. Since it was inside a chichi hotel, I hoped the salespeople would be less aggressive than those we had encountered on the streets. On the other hand, the shop looked small and shabby enough that I was hopeful I could find some souvenirs at reasonable prices. Buying souvenirs for family and friends is definitely not something any of us ever enjoyed, but it was a chore we had to endure on every trip. Even inside a plush palace hotel, bargaining went on as usual. I picked out a few knickknacks to bring home to friends. After a few minutes, the salesman and I agreed on a fifth of the price first quoted for the goods and both of us shook hands to mark a successful deal. Julian went back to the room to deposit the goods, while Fillip and I went looking for the hotel restaurant.

The restaurant's tables were arranged in a square around the outdoor courtyard. The courtyard, built in the Moorish style and located in the middle of the palace quarters, housed a fountain in the center. Beautifully carved arches outlined the almost invisible perimeters that divided outside from inside. We picked a table and the kids set off to examine the buffet tables. I sat down to order the wine and contemplated what we would need to put together a seder.

Passover Seder is not just a random dinner; it is a collection of prescribed food items, each symbolic of a part of the Exodus story. We had to improvise. The easiest to find was the *Karpas*, which are vegetables dipped in salt water and are symbolic of the tears of the Jewish people. I was able to pull some pickled hot peppers off the buffet table. Technically, these were dipped in salt water awhile back, but they were of the vegetable variety and their spiciness was sure to bring tears to our eyes.

Charoset was not too hard to find either. Under normal circumstances, *Charoset* would be a mixture of nuts and fruits mixed with wine. The mixture is symbolic of the mortar the Israelites were forced to use when they built structures for their Egyptian lords. We had red wine. With the addition of some honey and bananas, mixed with some soy nuts, the concoction looked close enough to mortar. Bitter herbs and vegetables (*Maror* and *Hazeret*) were a bit more difficult, as we were staying away from raw vegetables for health reasons. After a few walks around the buffet table, I finally pulled some hot vegetable relish. With the addition of some water mixed with salt, these would have to do. Obtaining a hard-boiled egg (*Baytzah*) was more of a challenge.

"Excuse me," I said, turning to one of the three turbaned, white-gloved waiters standing behind our table." I would like to order one hard-boiled egg, please."

"How many eggs Madame?"

"Just one, thank you."

"Not three, Madame?"

"No, one."

The waiter looked at our table intently. "How would you like that cooked, Madame?"

"Um, hard-boiled...boiled, until hard."

"All right, Madame."

The turbaned waiter disappeared into the darkness of the restaurant's interior. Exactly two minutes later, another appeared in his place.

"Did you order eggs, Madame?"

"Yes, thank you."

"How many eggs would you prefer, Madame? Three?"

I tried my best to remain calm. "No, just one, thank you."

"How would you like that egg prepared, Madame?"

"Hard-boiled, please. Um...please boil the egg until it is hard. Thank you."

I tried my best to not look at the kids. The two of them turned away from the waiters, and their bodies were shaking violently with laughter. At this point, some Austrian tourists who were seated nearby also were looking at us with curiosity.

Surprisingly, after a few minutes, our egg did arrive. And it was, indeed, hard-boiled. By then we were still missing a shank bone (*Zeroa*). The bone is symbolic of the tenth plague and the death of the firstborn Egyptian sons. The Israelites marked the doorposts of their homes with lamb's blood as a signal for death to pass over them. Considering our circumstances, I decided we would forgo the bone. If I had that much difficulty obtaining a hard-boiled egg, imagine the efforts required to explain a bone. Besides, I was worried that even if

I eventually succeeded in ordering the shank bone, the waiters would have me arrested for cult practices. All our food-gathering efforts and preparations mystified the staff, and at least four waiters at any given time stood right behind our table, staring at our little party with wide eyes and open mouths.

Finally, we had to have *matzah,* unleavened bread. When the Israelites fled Egypt, they had no time to let their dough rise. As a result, the only bread they ate was unleavened. To commemorate that, Jews all over the world eat unleavened bread for the eight-day duration of Passover. For our seder, we used a thin Indian wafer called *poppadom. Poppadom* would be my *matzah* for the next eight days, which just happened to be the remainder of our time in India.

The kids and I started to read from the story of the Exodus from a small *Haggadah* I had brought from home. As part of the ritual, we dutifully shared our *poppadom,* dipped vegetables in salt water, and took sips of red wine.

After I put away the book, we discussed the Jews' flight from Egypt, their fight for freedom, freedom in general, Jews' plight in general, the plight of the impoverished of India, and anything else that the story of Exodus led us to think about. We were so enthralled in our little Passover discussion that we almost did not notice the curious glances still thrown our way by the waiters and our fellow hotel guests. No one else was privy to our private holiday; only the three of us knew how special that night was. To this day, the seder we celebrated alone in the desert of Bikaner is the most memorable and meaningful to us. That night, the three of us really felt a sense of belonging. We belonged to an ancient people and we continued the legacy by carrying out an ancient tradition, even if we had to improvise most of it.

We were so caught up in our own little world that we did not at first pay attention to a mustached man in a white turban who had sat down at the far end of the courtyard and started playing a drum. After a few minutes, he was joined by a little girl. She was no more than ten or twelve years old and wore a traditional long multicolored skirt and a red top. She also wore thick layers of bright makeup. Long and heavy silver earrings fell all the way down to her shoulders and caused a lot of noise and sparkle as she danced.

At first, the little girl just danced to the beat of the drum. Then she picked up brightly colored clay jars off the ground and placed them on her head. One by one, she carefully stacked the jars until there were eight straight on top of her head and two hanging from the sides. As if that were not enough, when the jars were stacked, a woman approached, spread a large piece of white fabric in front of the girl, and placed shards of broken glass on top of the fabric. The girl kept dancing, without skipping a beat. Her bare feet were stepping on hundreds of pieces of razor-sharp glass. My boys were mesmerized; I was horrified. I imagined that the mustached man was the little girl's father and the woman with the glass was her mother. Would I be able to do that to my child? Would I have the nerve to train my child to cut her feet until they're numb enough to dance in front of a bunch of tourists who are so busy slicing their chicken at the time that they might not even take the time to look up and notice the local entertainment? What if that was my only means of earning an income? What if there were other children who had to be fed?

"Fillip, can you do me a favor and run to the room to get my wallet? I didn't bring it with me."

"You want to give her money, Mom?"

"Yes, I want to give her money."

After she survived the broken glass, the girl proceeded to dance with fire-lit hoops. The Austrians finally looked up from their beers and were clapping along with the drumbeat. Fillip was too shy to go give money to the girl but agreed to accompany his brother. Julian placed the money in the bucket next to the girl. She acknowledged the gesture by nodding her head and continued to dance. Julian and Fillip stepped aside into the shadow and remained there watching her until she finished her dance and left. Ours was the only money she received that night. The rest of the night, the kids were very somber and serious. It was almost as if the girl's burden had shifted onto them, and on some level, they felt the need to become more mature. Our evening was memorable and meaningful in more ways than one.

By the next morning, however, they were back to being twelve and ten again. While I was packing our suitcases for the next adventure, they were playing the same game of catch they have played since they were babies. It was harmless enough: forcefully throwing a pillow to each other with the hope that the opponent would not be able to catch it. For some reason, this exercise had irritated me for years, and this was especially true as I was busy attempting to leave the room on time to meet Sanjay, prevent any more bikini incidents, and generally be at peace while contemplating what I would be eating for the next eight days, considering my bread restrictions.

"Guys, can you please stop with the pillow?" I called out from the huge bath anteroom.

"Sorry, Mom." The pillow continued to fly.

"I mean it. Is it so difficult to stop?"

"Sorry, Mom." Once again, the words did not coincide with the actions, as I still heard the sound of the pillow hitting either the wall or the floor. Then I heard a different sound. I stopped packing.

"What was that?"

"Nothing, Mom."

I walked out of the anteroom and observed the bedroom. My sons were on either sides of the room, looking way too innocent. Something was not right. I walked around the room, but could not find anything out of place.

It was only as we were wheeling our suitcases out of the room that I noticed that one of the side lamps was shorter than the others. I walked over and saw that the shade was strategically placed over a pile of broken glass where only yesterday it had rested on a base in the shape of a vase. I started to chastise the kids, but after a few minutes just settled for collecting the pieces of glass into a large ice bucket and placing a large "careful, broken glass" note on top. The glimpse of maturity I had seen in my kids the night before would remain just that for now: a glimpse.

A busy *ghat* in Varanasi.

Author in Varanasi.

Julian (left) and Fillip (right) displaying their dirty feet on the walls of the Taj Mahal.

Fillip (left) and Julian (right) trying to blend into a temple in Gwalior.

Monkey Temple near Jaipur.

A splendid example of a Jaisalmer Haveli.

Julian (foreground) with village kids in the Thar Desert.

A sign in front of a temple in Johdpur.

One of the mutinous monkeys that caused us a brief delay on the road to Ranakpur.

Fillip (left) and Julian (right) pose for a farewell photo with Sanjay (middle) in front of the Ambassador in Udaipur.

Chapter 12

JAISALMER

Later that afternoon, we drove into Jaisalmer, which was as yellow as Jaipur was pink. All the buildings in the city were made of the same yellow sandstone. After a long drive through the desert, we were not going to do anything that day but enjoy a nice day at the pool.

Also at the pool were the Austrian couples we had seen the night before. Having recognized us, one of the women struck up a conversation, and she and I spent a good hour comparing notes on India, traveling with children, traveling in general, and children in particular. All in all, it was a lovely afternoon followed by a very late dinner. Having left the kids at the pool, I went up to the room to get an early start on my shower-hair-makeup routine. Unfortunately, every time I ran my blow dryer, I blew a circuit. Electricity would come back about five or ten minutes after that, only to go out again. We had a very late dinner by the poolside and were surprised by how cold a night in the desert could be.

The next morning did not start well. Having come down for breakfast, I was faced with the difficulty of finding a meal that was acceptable for me to eat during Passover. While my kids were happily munching on a variety of cereals, I had to find something Passover worthy. Eggs were no longer an option; having tried eggs in a number of hotels in India, I decided that I would rather eat a napkin, as it offered the same taste and fewer calories. The only other option was to have an Indian breakfast.

I'd like to preface this by noting that the kids and I love Indian food. Back in New York, we frequent Indian restaurants at least once or twice a month. For the first five days, at least, we were very happy to be in India enjoying its cuisine. After that, we quickly realized that restaurant menus were somewhat limited in their selection. To outsiders like us, *dal* was *dal*, regardless of the color of its lentils. Furthermore, waking up to the smell of curry was not something we were accustomed to. We desperately wanted some variety in our diet, even if it meant a Western-type omelet in the morning. So there I was in Jaisalmer, faced with a choice between breaking Passover or going hungry. I settled for a cup of coffee with a hard-boiled egg.

After breakfast, we set out for the fort of Jaisalmer. Constructed in the twelfth century CE, the fort is an enormous structure that looks like it's growing out of the mountain on which it is built. According to Sanjay, the fort is one of the few living forts left in India, with 60 percent of Jaisalmer's population living within its walls. Sanjay let us out in front of one of the gates leading into the fort, and we started our trek up the mountain and into the belly of Jaisalmer.

We fell in love with Jaisalmer at first sight. There was something about its tiny cobblestone streets surrounded on both sides by miniature doorways to shops and dwellings that felt medieval and untouched by time. Walking through the winding lanes, we could not help but be struck by the silence; outside of a few scooters, there were no vehicles. People were busy inside their homes. Shops were almost indistinguishable from the town walls. There was no horn honking, no traffic noise, and no bedlam, all of which we had become so accustomed to in the bigger cities. It was serene and peaceful, a town lost in space and time.

We explored every crevice of Jaisalmer; we climbed on every wall, peeked around every corner, and shopped in every shop. To this day, wrapped around my left ankle is a silver bracelet I bought in Jaisalmer. I found it in a tiny shop we had almost bypassed, as it was nestled behind a small wooden door. We walked up some stairs and found ourselves in silver haven. India's silversmiths are unique in their crafts and each town boasts its own style of jewelry. Julian was immediately drawn to a row of plain silver bands displayed on the wooden counter. I had my eye on the bracelets thrown into the bin beneath the rings. In keeping with local customs, we sat down to examine the merchandise the young salesman wished to show us. We went through dozens of trinkets until Julian settled on a small silver band and I chose a delicately carved ankle bracelet that jiggled when I walked and made noise when the tiny bells hanging from the lock bounced against each other. The salesman punched up the price on a large plastic solar calculator and turned it toward me. I conveyed obligatory shock at such high numbers, punched one-tenth of the amount in, and passed the calculator back to him. The owner expressed disappointment, took a few seconds to count some numbers in his head, (which he accompanied by rolling his eyes and silently moving his lips) then punched a counter offer and showed me the calculator. Likewise, I conveyed dismay, shook my head in distress, and punched more numbers before handing the calculator back to the salesman.

This charade went on for about five minutes, until the young man made a final plea for mercy by practically giving me the merchandise for free. I, likewise, explained my own monetary troubles and we agreed on one-fifth of the original asking price. I walked out of the store with a happy jiggle on my ankle.

"I wish he sold something with opal there as well," Fillip suddenly announced.

"Opal? Where is this coming from? And how do you even know what opal is?"

"It's my birthstone. I would like to have something with opal in it."

I was very surprised. Fillip, unlike his brother, did not freely spend money on trinkets; most of his purchases were well thought out and meaningful.

"If we see opal anywhere," I promised, "we'll get you something." We headed back to the car.

"I will take to see *havelis*, and then lunch," announced Sanjay.

Havelis are the sandstone mansions of Jaisalmer's wealthy merchants. These magnificent structures are so elaborately carved that they look as if they were made of lace. They stand next to each other, one flowing into the next, forming a wall of balconies and windows, doorways and staircases. We spent a good hour walking up and down the boulevards admiring these glorious homes.

"Ew!"

While Julian was admiring the balconies, he had not been watching where he walked. As a result, he had stepped into a pile of cow dung, which was a common sight on the streets of India. Julian's misfortune threw his brother into an uncontrollable fit of laughter. My pleas for Fillip's sense of compassion led nowhere; he could not stop laughing, which made his brother even more upset, but then karma stepped in (or rather Fillip stepped into it).

"Eww!" Now both of them were in the same stinking boat, and peace was restored. After a few minutes of frantically scrubbing their flip-flops against the pavement, I led the two stink bombs back to the car so we could head to lunch.

We pulled onto a residential street and stopped in front of a second-floor restaurant. The restaurant was spread out on the patio, covered by a straw roof held up by thick canes of bamboo. The waiter was very particular about placing us at a certain table, even though we were the only clients in the restaurant. We sat down at a long wooden table covered by a cotton tablecloth. Judging by the deep brown stains on the tablecloth, it also had served as a napkin to many diners. Ten days earlier, such total disregard for hygiene would have put us in a total frenzy. Back in Jaisalmer, however, we just gave each other knowing looks and shrugged. *Ye hai India.* Our silverware matched the tablecloth, so we wiped our knives and forks with the edges of the tablecloth and enjoyed a wonderful lunch accompanied by the steady buzzing of flies swarming around our table.

The place Sanjay took us to next completely baffled us. It was in the middle of the desert, yet there were some structures ahead, and to walk up to those structures we had to pay admission fees. We could not understand Sanjay's explanation of where we were. The sign ahead announced that we were entering the site of Bada Bagh, a collection of royal cenotaphs going back to the sixteenth century. A cenotaph is a memorial tomb that is empty, as the person's remains were buried elsewhere. Bada Bagh was a small town of memorials. Its elaborate cupolas, built on intricately carved arches, looked almost like palaces that suddenly had been abandoned.

At first, we wandered the deserted town alone. The kids jumped on and off the walls of the tombs that once were revered by royalty. After about ten minutes, we were joined by a goat. The lonely white goat seemed to be totally oblivious to the fact that this was the desert. He lethargically poked his nose at the ground in the attempts to find food. Apparently he did, because his jaw did not stop moving, and his eyes opened and closed in rhythm with his chewing mouth. We soon realized that the goat was accompanied by two "shepherds." The two kids escorting the goat looked like siblings and were no older than five and seven. Neither of them had any shoes, and their clothes were old, dusty, and worn. It seemed that they had found their daily entertainment in my sons and me. They would run around a wall or a hill from which they could observe our little outing unnoticed— or so they thought. It wasn't long until my kids were playing a silent game of hide-and-seek with the two shepherds. Julian and Fillip would hide behind a wall or an archway, and the kids would come close. Then my sons would jump out from their hideaway, sending the shepherds into hiding.

As we left Bada Bagh, the two young boys stood on the hill watching us go. It was only after we got into the car and started to pull away that the kids finally turned and headed back in the direction from which they had come.

It was still early and we had time to make one more stop: the Gadi Sagar Lake. Gadi Sagar is actually a man-made reservoir that used to serve as the only water source for Jaisalmer. The lake is surrounded by beautiful temples, shrines, and *ghats*. Boats were parked all along the shores of the lake, indicating tourist interest. There were no people, however, to work the boats, so even if we had wanted to, we could not have hired one. We approached the lake through a gate and saw a wall of trees; it looked almost surreal considering the desert surrounding this place. We walked toward the trees and stopped short; a herd of water buffalo was crossing our path. Not paying the slightest attention to us, the animals leisurely strolled by, shaking their tails lazily to ward off the swarm of bugs accompanying their march.

"Mom, you did see that, right?" Julian asked in disbelief.

"Well they are quite big, you know," I responded. "They would be difficult to miss."

"Just like that," Fillip said in awe, "water buffalos in the middle of the city!"

"Just like that," I repeated, thinking we were caught in some surreal universe. Further along, four dogs made their bed under the carved stone canopy of what looked like a small stage. All of them found such pleasure in their sleep in the shade that only one of them bothered to open an eye as we passed by.

As we headed back from the lake, we had to pause to give way to a heard of oxen. "Yep!" I repeated, "Just like that, in the middle of the city."

Back at the hotel, we were walking to our room when we were stopped in our tracks by another phenomenon: a pomegranate tree. My kids love pomegranates, but having grown up in a city, they had never given much thought to where their favorite fruit came from. Seeing a tree with pomegranates hanging off its branches threw them into another fit of excitement, not unlike what some may experience upon seeing a UFO. I suppose we were carrying on about the pomegranates a bit too long and a bit too loudly, which drew the attention of our Austrian neighbors. They joined us in the admiration of the Indian flora and we carried on some more conversation about the tree. Two Indian gardeners, who were watering the flowers nearby, stopped their work and stared at us. They said something to each other and laughed. I agreed with them. How ridiculous we must have seemed: grown people creating such fuss and commotion over something as simple and natural as a pomegranate.

That evening, the kids and I had drinks on the roof of our hotel overlooking Jaisalmer. I was sipping a glass of wine while the kids enjoyed some local juice concoction served in cocktail glasses. The warm desert breeze brought out the giggles as we discussed what to buy my husband for his upcoming birthday. Every suggestion—from a pomegranate to a goat to a turban—was accompanied by a fit of laughter and further ideas that were even sillier and more outrageous. There was something about the desert air that was so alluring and almost hypnotic, or perhaps it was Jaisalmer and our reluctance to leave that kept us on that roof for over two hours. We only got up when Julian's stomach, devoid of food, started talking to us, reminding us that it was not just our souls that needed to be fed.

That night I dreamed that I was in the desert. The sand was lit up by the afternoon sun and looked as if it were aflame. I couldn't move. My feet were firmly planted in the sand as if I had become part of the sand dune.

Chapter 13

THAR DESERT

The next morning, we planned to head into the desert to spend a day in a camel camp. The camp was only a short drive away from Jaisalmer, and I was able to pack in the morning at leisure. The kids went down to the pool, and I told them I would join them when I was done. I had been looking forward to soaking in the sun's rays, but then the kids ran back into the room.

"That's it? I wasn't expecting to see you for at least an hour!" I exclaimed in surprise.

"Mom, the water is freezing!"

"Freezing? Are you crazy?" Then I remembered we were in a desert—hot days, cold nights. We had a long breakfast and went out to meet Sanjay in front of the hotel. We began our drive into the heart of the Thar Desert.

Spanning more than 77,000 square miles, Thar is the world's seventh largest desert. Parts of it lie in Pakistan, which was quite apparent as we drove along the Indian-Pakistani border to find the camp. Camp Mirvana itself was a big surprise to us. Having the word "camp" in its name automatically predisposed us to be ready for the worst, as I had visions of summer camps playing out in my head. Luckily, Mirvana was nothing like I had imagined. Surrounded by nothing but sand dunes, the camp itself was a beautiful lush oasis. Each room was an individual stone bungalow with all the creature comforts one could ask for: comfortable beds, toilets, and showers. While Julian and I were examining the washroom, Fillip discovered a hidden gem: a window seat. The seat was built into a protruding bungalow window and was covered by a soft thin mattress. The enclave came complete with throw pillows and a curtain shielding it from the rest of the room.

"I'm sleeping here," declared Fillip before Julian and I had a chance to even see what he was talking about. "This is a perfect bed and I'm sleeping here tonight." Fillip looked absolutely ecstatic and I was not going to ruin his excitement. Besides, he was small enough to perfectly fit into the window seat.

After we unpacked, we strolled over to the main office to make arrangements for our camel ride into the desert. The camp looked deserted. "Are we the only ones here?" I inquired of a mustached manager at the office.

"For the moment, Madame, yes," he replied before asking me to sign paperwork.

"The camels will be waiting for you at sundown, Madame," he announced after the papers were signed and fees paid.

"Um, would you be a bit more specific, please?" I felt silly asking but didn't want to miss our ride.

"You could come about five-thirty or six o'clock, Madame," he responded. "Would you like to have some lunch now?"

"That would be nice, thank you," I replied, and we set off for what looked like a straw hut at the other end of the camp. As soon as we left the office, we saw a tour bus pull up in front of the camp entrance. The silent tranquility of the camp immediately turned into a noisy bustle accompanied by loud laughter and songs. Hungry French tourists were heading toward our restaurant, and at that moment, the manager put on the radio. The sounds of Indian music blasting through the speakers mixed with French pop songs created a loud yet festive disharmony. We were glad the rowdy tourists were just passing through.

Back in the restaurant, the French were already busy choosing their meals. We sat next to them, at the only available table, and reviewed the menu. Everything on the restaurant menu looked great. Then again, we were hungry. Unfortunately, Fillip had been complaining of an upset stomach all morning, and as I went through a list of foods he should not have, he quickly became disillusioned and just ordered some rice, while Julian and I enjoyed a scrumptious meal of *dal*, chicken, vegetables, and rice. Another treat of the restaurant was its dessert. This was the first time the kids and I had seen and tasted *gulab jamun*. The dessert is made of doughy balls soaked in sugary syrup. Sometimes, it is also covered in edible gold or silver foil. For the remainder of our stay in India, every time Julian saw *gulab jamun* on the menu, it was a sure choice. Often, Fillip joined him. But on that afternoon in Mirvana Desert Camp, poor Fillip just looked on as Julian and I all but licked our fingers clean devouring the delicacy.

We had some free time after lunch, so the kids and I went to the pool. By that time, the French were long gone and the camp became peaceful and quiet. The only sounds that broke the tranquility of the oasis were the loud splashes the kids made when jumping into the water. Their dives were soon interrupted by a hornet's nest that the insects had made right next to the diving board's steps. The boys addressed this by deciding to jump in at the opposite end of the pool, instead. Even though they never came close enough to the nest, either the sounds of their jumps or the waves of the pool stirred up the hornets every time. The hornets' angry buzzing quickly became very unnerving. Furthermore, the water was icy cold and after about thirty minutes of running in and out of the pool, the children began shivering violently and their lips had turned blue. I suggested they sit out in the sun for a few minutes to warm up. Exactly two minutes later, Fillip suddenly jumped up and started to sprint in the direction of our hut. "I have to go to the bathroom!" he yelled at us as he ran. "It's my stomach!"

Julian and I promptly got up, gathered our things, and left the pool to help Fillip.

It took us twenty minutes to clean the hut's bathroom, which my ten-year-old had not quite reached. He was so embarrassed by the incident that Julian and I spent another thirty minutes just calming him down and explaining that there was nothing he could have done differently. Within an hour, the whole incident was behind us, and, as I had promised the kids earlier, I set out to play Ping-Pong with them.

The Ping-Pong table stood on a concrete slab next to one of the huts. The location was very unfortunate, as one of the edges of the table was only about two feet away from the edge of the slab. If a ball was not hit, it went over the edge and someone had to jump down to the ground to chase it down the sloping surface. While two of us played, the third person waited to play the winner. To make our lives easier, one of us had to stand on the ground to catch loose balls. It was also at that game that my kids learned a new word: ricochet. Because the long side of the old table was right next to a wall, almost every time we hit the ball a bit off to the side, it ricocheted right back onto the table. The kids would make up rules on ricochets as we went along. Ping-Pong was never so much fun.

By six o'clock, two camels were waiting for us at the camp's entrance. Both were decked out in camel finery, complete with tinsel, bells, and glitter. Two men in worn beige tunics and large red turbans accompanied the camels. Both men sported absurdly long mustaches that curled up at both ends. We decided the mustaches were decoys for their mouths, which were missing most of the front teeth. Come to think of it, we weren't sure why the men were there. The camel in the front was led by a boy of about fourteen. The camel in the back followed the other's lead. The turbaned men walked alongside our procession. I let Julian ride by himself while Fillip and I shared the second camel. The kids had never ridden camels before, and the initial jerking motion of the rising camel (toe-knee-heel) threw them into a mild panic, followed by nervous laughter. I held onto Fillip and talked Julian through moving in line with the camel as the turbaned men giggled and exchanged disdainful glances. I didn't think explaining to them that there are no camels in New York City would rectify the situation.

"OK, Mom, this is way high!" My brave twelve-year-old was scared to be seven feet off the ground.

"It's not that high, Julian," I said, trying to reassure him.

"Are you kidding, Mom? This is scary!" Fillip chimed in.

"Do you want to get off? Should we just forget about the camels?"

"Well, we're already on them."

So off we went. The desert was golden with the setting sun. We were alone, it seemed, for miles and miles: no roads, no people, no sign of dwellings. Every now and then, we would hear animal sounds that we could not identify. Our guides did not speak English so we let our imaginations run away with us; we thought we heard every predator we had ever read about, from wolves to coyotes to tigers. The only animals we saw, however, were dead ones; every now and then, we passed by a skull or the bones of what looked like a camel or a gazelle.

After about a half hour, we approached a village that reminded me of places I had read about in *National Geographic*. There were no roads. Mud brick huts were scattered randomly amid the desert sands and occasional thorny bushes. Barefoot children herded goats. An old woman squatted next to a water well, whose wheel was turned by two white oxen. At the sight of the camels, the young herders perked up. Most of them abandoned their animal charges to follow our little procession. Our turbaned guides feebly attempted to chase away the children with long sticks they had picked up along the way. The kids sidestepped the sticks, only to circle right back to our camels. By the time we entered the middle of the village, our entourage had become quite sizeable. We were surrounded by locals on all sides when our guides halted the camels and gestured for us to get off. Not knowing what to expect or do, we remained standing in the middle of the road when one of the guides motioned us to follow him. We did. What was easily half of the village population followed us. We walked into a tiny front yard of a hut. A toothless middle-aged woman in a bright purple sari motioned us to sit on a wooden bench covered by a dark brown throw. The kids sat down and were immediately swallowed by a crowd of people. Some were gesturing, some whispering into each other's ears. Others just stared with their mouths wide open.

"Now what, Mom?" asked Julian quietly.

"I have no idea," I responded. "I guess we stay here for a few minutes and then go back?"

The woman in a bright purple sari reappeared from the house with a pot of *masala chai* in one hand and a metal mug in another. She silently gestured the chai offering to us.

"*Dhan'yav da,*" I responded, "*nahim.*" "Thank you, but no."

Julian and Fillip were now looking at me intently for instructions. I assumed an absurdly wide grin. "Don't even think it," I hissed through the grin, "You can't take chances with water here."

"*Nahim, nahim,*" echoed the kids politely.

I wished I could walk around to explore the village, but the crowd surrounding us made it impossible. All we could do was remain in one spot until I found one of our guides and motioned him to come back. It took awhile to get going, as our teen camel guide was already sitting down next to one of the huts drinking *chai* and chatting it up with one of the village residents. The teen clearly was not yet ready to depart and only got up reluctantly after a brief spat with our turbaned friend. It was almost with a sigh of relief that we climbed back onto the camels to go back into the desert.

We only got as far as the other end of the village when we were stopped once again, this time by a crowd of young men in their twenties and thirties, dressed to the max. The men sported bright polyester dress shirts with brown or gray slacks. Some had flowers in their hair. I heard a loud commotion from a crowd of women standing near the young men. The sounds kept getting louder and I finally identified them as sobbing. I looked in the direction of the commotion and saw a large crowd of women dressed in bright saris and flower gar-lands. They were crowding around a young woman who was shaking with sobs. Suddenly it dawned on me: "Kids, we're in the middle of a wedding."

"Wedding? How do you know?"

"There's the crying bride."

"And here is the groom," added Julian, nodding to a young man near our camel. By all indications, this had to have been the lucky chap whose special day this was. Not only was he dressed, like his friends, in a bright flowered shirt with slacks, but he also wore a disproportionately tall black hat, which almost resembled that of a nineteenth-century cossack hat. Once again, we were surrounded by a crowd.

While the women's party was busy consoling the bride, who was about to leave her family home, the men's party found us much more entertaining. Some tried to show off their language skills: "Hallo, Hallo, friend." Others were staring. Then another young man, who up until then had been standing next to the woman's party, turned to us, and we burst out laughing. In his hands he held a camera, and instead of photographing the wedding, he de-cided to start photographing us. The scene looked surreal. It didn't help that some women consoling the bride started throwing dis-approving looks at the young men. The crowd remained until our turbaned guides decided not to ruin their relationship with the womenfolk. They picked up thin sticks off the ground and, waving their arms in front of them, proceeded to make their way through the crowd. Some of the men continued to follow us through the village roads. By the time we reached the desert, we were finally on our own again.

The kids were no longer freaked out by the bumpy stride of the camels and we were able to sit back and enjoy the sunset. It was one of the most magnificent sights I have seen—ever. At first, the sun hovered low above the horizon. The yellow sand reflected the sun's rays and the desert became blinding with light. The lower the sun descended, the bigger it became; no longer golden, it was a giant crimson orb that rested on the horizon. The horizon started to swallow it very slowly, inch by inch, until there was just a hint of light right above the ground. And then it was gone.

We rode back in silence, afraid to interrupt this intimate moment between the desert and the sun. When we returned to the camp, Sanjay was playing basketball with the camp staff. Once we were spotted, the game came to an abrupt end.

"Good evening, Madame, did you enjoy?" Sanjay seemed embarrassed to be seen doing anything but his work. His teammates, likewise, looked uncomfortable with the fact that hotel guests had seen them at leisure. I felt terrible. Unfortunately, all of my pleas to continue the game led to nothing. The game was over.

The mustached manager was waiting for us in front of the office hut. "Will you be showering, Madame?"

To be honest, the question threw me off. It's not every day that hotel staff takes an interest in your hygiene habits.

"Um, yes," I responded reluctantly.

"And the children, Madame? Will they also wish to shower?"

"Um, yes, they will."

"Very well, Madame. We will turn on the water heater. Please allow about thirty minutes for the water to heat."

It made perfect sense to me. *Ye hai India,* darling, I thought. Of course it would take thirty minutes for the water to heat.

"Will you prefer your dinner before or after the shower?"

"After, please. Where will dinner be served?"

"In front of your room, Madame."

That was something new. The kids and I proceeded to the room and sat out our half hour before showers. We were dusty and smelly and every minute seemed like an eternity. The kids played cards; I read. Every five minutes or so, someone went into the bathroom to feel the water. After about fifty minutes, the water was still only luke-warm. We finally decided that waiting for anything hotter than that would mean eating dinner at midnight. Once again, we settled for lukewarm showers.

I was still drying my hair when Fillip stuck his head outside the hut. "Mom, there's a man outside carrying a grill to our room," he announced.

"Why do you think it's meant for our room?" I inquired.

"Because he just placed it right next to it."

A few minutes later, Fillip peeked outside again. "Now he's making a fire," he said.

For the next half hour, while I was getting dressed, the kids went in and out of the room and reported the goings-on to me:

"Now he threw some rocks on the grill."

"He is waving a piece of newspaper in front of the grill."

"He is pouring something on the grill."

"Another man just came and put a table in front of our room."

"He brought chairs and candles."

By the time I came out of the room, the stars were bright in the sky, the grill was lit, and the table was set. Momentarily, a white-gloved waiter appeared in front of the table. The kids ordered some lamb and chicken; I settled for vegetables and white wine. Then the cooking started. The smell of grilled food that emanated from the grill was beyond description. Considering that we hadn't eaten since early that afternoon, we were salivating from the smell and the smoke. Then the appetizers started coming. The assortment of salads we ordered was enough to feed the village we had just visited. It was a never-ending procession of curried vegetables, breads, sauces, and dips. This was accompanied by a full bottle of wine. By the time our main course arrived, we were full. We only ate because the freshly grilled meats and vegetables were prepared to perfection and because the warm April night was so heavenly that we didn't want the day to end. We discussed everything that happened that day, from our game of Ping-Pong to our hornet-filled pool to the camel ride and the village wedding. We laughed till our stomachs hurt and our heads pulsated. Then we wondered what new adventure awaited us the next day.

Life was good.

Chapter 14

JODHPUR

We were still full the following morning so we skipped breakfast and headed straight for Jodhpur. The second largest city in Rajasthan, Jodhpur is also known as the Blue City, as many houses around its fort are painted sky blue. It was still early afternoon when we neared Jodhpur so we headed straight for its fort, the Mehrangarh Fort, located on the outskirts of town. Perched four hundred feet above the town of Jodhpur, the fort was certainly the most imposing of the those we had seen. It was also one of the best preserved. The fort museum did an outstanding job curating its rooms and corridors to replicate the times of its former glory. From the armory to the art and the musical instruments, each room was meticulously restored, brightly lit, and well documented by the strategically placed signs.

The fort originally had seven gates; the one through which we entered was the Elephant Gate. Its narrow passage contained iron spikes on both sides of the entry to prevent elephant attacks. What was more unnerving to us, however, was a cement block with fifteen hand imprints. These belonged to the royal *satis*, wives who had immolated themselves on the funeral pyres of their dead husbands. Perhaps because the hands were so small and delicate or perhaps because they were each different, the horrific scenes of cremation played out like cinema reels in my head. Luckily, my children brought me back to Earth.

"Mom, I'm very hungry," declared Julian, ignoring the visible emotional effect the handprints were having on his mother.

"It's only eleven-thirty. You want to eat now?"

"Yes, Mom, now."

We walked into the nearest restaurant, which was right inside the fort. It was not until Fillip had his fill of *dal* and Julian had feasted on *gulab jamun* that we were able to proceed with sightseeing. The highlight of our tour that afternoon was an ancient man in a huge turban and an equally huge gray mustache, which curled at both sides. The man was sitting cross-legged in a shallow niche of the palace wall. He was staring straight ahead and sucking in big gulps of smoke from a glass hookah. The sign in front of him had only one word: opium. Judging by his glassy stare, I didn't think it was for demonstration purposes only.

It was only a short drive from the fort to Jaswant Thada, the traditional cremation ground of Maharaja Jaswant Singh II, the thirty-third ruler of Jodhpur. The memorial is a truly brilliant example of Indian architecture. It is built entirely of white marble carved into polished white stones. When the sun is reflected off the polished stones, the monument seems to be almost ablaze in a warm golden glow.

A large sign posted at the bottom of the stairs leading up to the entrance instructed us to remove our shoes. We obliged and quickly found ourselves jumping from spot to spot to get to the top as the temperature outside easily reached 40°C, making the beautiful stones hot as coals. We were the only visitors to the site and truly enjoyed exploring the splendid structure, as well as the view from its hilly location.

It took a while for Sanjay to find our hotel in Jodhpur. The hotel was in an old city that was located behind an ancient wall. Driving into the city, we were once again surrounded by the hustle and bustle of an Indian metropolis. It took quite some time to navigate the narrow streets of Jodhpur and make our way to the hotel, which was on one of the more thoroughly veiled alleyways. Hotel Pal Haveli was hidden behind a market thoroughfare in a residential part of Jodhpur. It was once the private residence of Thakur Umaid Karanji, who accompanied a Maharaja from Gujarat to Jodhpur. In appreciation of the services rendered, Thakur was awarded a tiny hamlet of Pal, about fifteen kilometers from Jodhpur. Later, the family moved to the city and built this *haveli* (palace), which had become a hotel only a few years before our arrival. It was still managed by Thakur's descendants.

A *haveli* is made up of numerous corridors and passages, some of which lead to dead ends. We know that because right after dropping off our bags, we set out to explore the building. The first thing that struck us about the architecture of the hotel was what seemed to be a total lack of planning. Rooms were nestled on top of each other without any pattern or design. One corridor might lead to a room that leads to another room and then a long passageway with nothing on either side. On the floor above, the layout could be completely reversed. Furthermore, the staircases of the hotel were the steepest I have ever experienced. The steps were almost at a seventy-degree angle and were spaced as high as three feet from one another. After about fifteen minutes of scaling the staircases of the hotel, we left to see the town. As soon as we turned the corner from our quiet residential alleyways, the city hit us with all its loud and powerful might.

The two-square-mile radius surrounding our hotel was one giant market square. Immediately adjacent to our hotel was a bazaar with clearly defined sections of stands, each displaying wares of a particular kind; there was a spice section, which was next to a vegetable section, which ran into a souvenir section that ended with housewares. Past that, however, it was a free-for-all. Everywhere the eye could see was just a quagmire of stalls, carrying everything from food to shoe soles (that's right, no shoes, just piles and piles of rubber and leather soles of all sizes and shapes). After about an hour's stroll, we headed back. We only walked in a circle twice before figuring out which street to make a turn onto for Pal Haveli.

Exhausted by all the walking that day, we made our way back to the hotel and headed straight for the restaurant. The restaurant was located on a rooftop, which required us to climb three steep flights of stairs, leaving us breathless and worn out. We happily made our way to the nearest table and ordered drinks. After a few sips of wine and yogurt lassies, we finally relaxed and looked around. While we were enjoying our beverages, the city seemed to be rushing to finish yet another busy day. Rickshaws were weaving through crowds of people and livestock. The sound of car horns permeated the twilight. Loud thumps of dropping shop gates sent dozens of sleeping monkeys scattering around nearby buildings to escape the noise. Right below our hotel was a large water reservoir with three feeble fountains in the middle. The water in the reservoir was neon green and heaps of garbage floated along its edges. A group of young boys, naked except for their underwear, were diving into the water from the high walls of the reservoir.

"Did we not take our camera here?" It was a rhetorical question on my part. We generally did not take a camera to dinner.

"No, Mom, we didn't."

"Julian, would you mind going to the room to get it?"

"Are you kidding, Mom? I'm so happy we made it all the way up here; there is no way I am going down those stairs only to climb more stairs to get to the room." Seeing the horrified expression on his face, I decided not to pursue this further.

"Fillip?"

"What he said!" shrieked Fillip before I even had a chance to finish.

"Oh, well," I sighed. "I can use some exercise."

I retrieved the camera and was back on the roof within twenty minutes as the stars started to appear in the graying sky. The car horns had almost subsided, the rickshaws receded, and the monkeys were calmly and comfortably perched on nearby rooftops.

"*Allahu Akhbar*!" rang out from the loudspeakers of a distant minaret. "*Allahu Akhbar*!"

And then the city fell asleep. The stillness of the night was interrupted only by an occasional monkey jumping from building to building or the three of us passing a cell phone from one to another, retelling the events of the day to my husband in New York.

Chapter 15

RANAKPUR

After a brief stop at the royal palace in the morning, we were off to Ranakpur. It was only a little while after we left Jodhpur that the topography radically changed. We were no longer driving through the desert; instead, we were making our way through a very green valley up the mountains. This wasn't camel country. The lush vegetation accompanying our drive offered us magnificent views of lakes and mountainsides populated by exotic birds and creatures straight out of *National Geographic*. We spent most of the ride playing "guess the creature," though we had no trouble identifying the troop of monkeys we encountered in the middle of the road.

The monkeys apparently didn't care that we had to get to Ranakpur. They were leisurely grooming each other in the middle of both lanes of the country road, and not even the car horn that Sanjay dutifully hit four times convinced the creatures to leave the traffic zone. In a show of protest to the horn, three of the evil beasts jumped on top of our Ambassador and proceeded to display overt signs of belligerence. For the first three minutes, we were somewhat amused; after that, we were at a loss. We all got out of the car to plead with the insolent creatures, but it was to no avail. We had no food with which to bribe them. Sanjay picked up a long thin stick off the road to try to shoo them away, but all it did was pique their interest; now even the sleeping members of the troop woke up and came closer to examine the curious object in Sanjay's hand. The kids waved their arms around wildly. That further piqued the monkeys' interest. The big help from me came in the form of sporadic shouts to the kids instructing them not to get any closer to the animals. Eventually, the monkeys became bored with us. One by one, they migrated from the road to the branches of the nearby tree. We were free to move along.

We arrived at Ranakpur Hill Resort to check in and drop off our bags. While I was filling out a stack of forms at the concierge desk, Sanjay reappeared to announce with a smile that the hotel had a room for him as well. That made the kids and me just as happy, knowing that he doesn't have to wander too far and could take a well-deserved rest in the evening. We didn't even bother changing our clothes when we got to the room. We threw our bags on the floor, took a quick facilities break, and were right back out to meet Sanjay on the way to see the Ranakpur temples.

The temples of Ranakpur owe their fame to their intricate and superb architectural style. They are part of the five major pilgrimages of the Jains. The Chaumjkha Temple (the Four-Faced Temple) is the main one in the complex and dates back to the fifteenth century. Built in marble, the temple has twenty-nine halls and is supported by more than fourteen hundred columns, no two of which are carved in the same fashion. These columns are known to change their color from golden to pale blue, depending on the time of day. It took sixty-five years to build this work of art.

We arrived at the complex in the early afternoon, which is the hottest time of the day. Taking off our shoes, we hopped to the worn-out brown rug thrown loosely onto the marble staircase leading to the entrance to the temple. Once inside, we were able to leisurely explore the beautiful building. A group of schoolboys in long slacks and tucked-in dress shirts followed us for awhile and giggled, pointing their fingers at my sons. Bothersome at first, they quickly faded into the background as we refused to let their presence distract us from enjoying ourselves. Eventually, the boys grew tired of us and fell behind as we moved on from hall to hall. Julian and Fillip hopped from column to column, imitating numerous deity images seen in the temple. Fillip, whose squatting skills and stamina rivaled any Indian-born child, would do so while crouching between columns, throwing Julian and me into fits of laughter.

After spending a few hours at the temple complex, we went back to the hotel. Ranakpur is little more than a village hidden deep in the woods. There were no other sights to be seen, so we headed for the pool.

While we were changing into our bathing suits, the kids happened to catch a game of cricket on the television. The sport was new to them; they had never heard of it back in the States. I am not sure if it was the sport itself or the hype surrounding that particular match, but the kids decided to try their hand at it. They didn't have any equipment, so they settled for some sticks and an old ball they picked up in the grass next to the pool.

I made myself comfortable under the hot blazing sun and tried to read. There was something in the air, however, that kept me from concentrating on the pages. I couldn't figure out at first what was standing in the way between the book and me. Then I realized: it was a smell. There was a very powerful smell right next to me that was intoxicating, yet familiar. I got up and walked over to the bushes behind the pool chair. There it was: jasmine. I had never seen jasmine before, but the scent was unmistakable. I backed up my pool chair into the white flowers and called the kids over.

"Smell this," I commanded as the two of them approached. Both wore sour pusses, as I had interrupted their game.

"You called us over for this?"

"Yes. You have to smell this."

"Wow! What is it?" Fillip was smitten at first whiff.

"I told you, it's jasmine."

"How do you know what jasmine looks like, Mom?"

"I don't. I mean I didn't, until now. But the smell is so distinct that you can't mistake it for anything else."

After a few more whiffs, the kids went back to the game. I tried to finish another chapter in my book, all the while turning my head from left to right to stick my nose into the flowering bush.

The kids came back for a quick splash in the pool before going to the room to get ready for dinner. "We have a surprise for you," announced Julian. "It's in the room."

"You didn't break anything again, did you?" I asked suspiciously.

"No, it's a nice surprise," Fillip reassured me. "You'll see."

He was right; it was the nicest surprise I could have expected. Standing on the coffee table back in our room was a bouquet of the most beautiful flowers I had ever seen, arranged neatly in a drinking glass. I could not name them, but they were very colorful and exotic. Best of all, they were crowned by none other than a jasmine flower as a centerpiece. I felt tears welling up in my eyes.

"This is the nicest thing anyone has ever done for me. Where did you find them?"

"We picked them in the bushes next to the fence where we played," explained Julian.

"We saw you carrying on about the jasmine and decided to pick them for you," Fillip added. "Do you like them?"

"I absolutely love them," I said. It remains the loveliest bouquet I have ever received.

"We knew you would," the kids said; they were proud of themselves.

"The only problem," I noted, "is that we can't take the bouquet with us."

"We can't?" Now Julian sounded heartbroken. "But we picked it for you."

"I know," I said, "we'll take photos of it. This way I'll always have it."

"Good idea, Mom," agreed the kids. I proceeded to take numerous photos at dozens of different angles and distances, not that I needed to; I can always close my eyes and remember every detail about that small but perfect bouquet. I can still smell it.

That night, we had dinner in the hotel garden at a table set up in front of our room. The night was exceptionally starry and we spent a good two hours discussing the events of the day and laughing at the Bollywood radio station blaring its musical selections at us until they pulsated in our heads. I kept smelling jasmine.

Checking out of a hotel was never a simple affair in India. Piles of papers had to be signed, passports examined, cards swiped again and again. The concierge at the Ranakpur Hill Resort finally took pity on us and suggested we wait in an adjacent library while the hotel staff gathered our luggage and put their papers in order. We gladly obliged and crossed the outside hall to situate ourselves on the two large comfortable sofas placed along the walls of the library. I had just reached out to grab a magazine from a coffee table between the sofas when I heard a shriek. I looked up. Julian was sitting perfectly upright and frozen in the sofa across from me. He moved his eyes to the right of me as if to direct my attention to something. I immediately turned my head, only to let out a similar shriek: sitting next to my sofa was something of a cross between a dog and a yeti.

As I tried to ascertain what the creature might be, the creature's twin slowly strolled into the room and stretched out in the hallway between us and the door. We were now surrounded by two creatures of enormous proportions that were blocking our entrance and exits; we were trapped. We remained motionless in our seats, staring at the creatures. They were seemingly Great Danes but they were huge. The smaller one, the female, was the size of a small calf while her companion, a male, would easily tower over a newborn elephant. I pondered how we could make our escape. Our passage was blocked by the dogs and we remained still so as not to draw attention to ourselves.

"Now what, Mom?" asked Julian, without moving his lips.

"Not sure," I answered, in the same manner.

"They seem friendly," offered Fillip

"They do," I agreed, not sure that I believed it.

"I'm not getting up until they leave," warned Julian, and I knew he meant it.

"Perhaps, I can get up to distract them?" I wondered aloud, once again not believing my own words.

"And then what?" hissed Fillip, also afraid to move his lips. "We run while they eat you?"

"I think we are overreacting," I tried to reassure everyone. "They look like two friendly puppies." The dogs looked more like the hounds of the Baskervilles, but I didn't want to scare the kids any more than they already were.

We proceeded to have a plan of action debate. We spoke in very hushed voices without moving our heads or lips. The dogs seemed to not even be paying attention to our panic. Then, just as I was about to hatch a diversion-and-escape plan, the female got up and walked out of the room. The male followed her as nonchalantly as he had walked in. We bolted out of the library. We were only able to relax when we were comfortably seated in the safety of our Ambassador and Sanjay hit the gas pedal.

Chapter 16

UDAIPUR

It was only a few hours' drive to Udaipur. The newly wooded road took us through the mountains. Driving through the narrow winding roads gave us an exhilarating high as we looked down on the clouds beneath us. We didn't even notice the time until we finally descended into a valley. As we were passing a tall palm tree with a layer of something dark under its peak, Julian screamed out, "Bats! Did you see that? Wow!"

Sanjay promptly hit the brakes and the car backed up to the tree. All four of us got out of the car and looked straight up. The top of the tree was blanketed with a thick layer of large furry bats. The bats were hanging upside down from the tree's top branches; from a distance, they looked like part of the tree. The bats were a solid mass of ghastly dark fur as they swayed in a dreamy unison. Periodically, the wind would knock one of them down. The fallen bat would momentarily wake from its slumber only to fly right back to the tree branch and close its eyes again. The kids wanted to stay longer; I badly wanted to leave. The thought of having to rip one of these repulsive rodents out of my hair made me shiver. Sanjay and I went back into the car, and the kids stayed behind for a few moments longer before following us into the Ambassador.

A few minutes later, we stopped again. This time it was a well that stopped us in our tracks. Two large white oxen walked around in a slow circle, drawing water from the well. The oxen were manned by a little boy, no older than six, in a dirty beige tunic. The boy squatted a few feet away from the oxen in the shadow of a tree and periodically whipped the beasts with a thin long branch. Every time the stick hit the animals, they blinked and jerked their ears, as if shooing away an annoying bug. Nothing about that scene indicated twenty-first century. Alas, we had not just traveled to a different country; we had been transported into a different era.

After a final stop for lunch, we arrived in Udaipur. Udaipur is a charming, sleepy town complete with cobblestone alleys and old winding streets flanked by small shops selling souvenirs and other useless tourist wares. We didn't waste any time and set off to explore this small gem right after dropping off our bags at the hotel. At first, we took the obligatory tourist route and found our way to the royal palace. Compared to the numerous forts and palaces we saw along the way, the Udaipur palace didn't stand a chance. It wasn't that it was smaller or less splendid than others, it was just that we wished to step away from the crowds to see the real attraction that Udaipur had to offer: itself. So, we stepped off the main thoroughfare and went into the first side street we crossed. The detour was worthwhile. There, in front of us, perched high atop a steep staircase, was a temple. It was small and serene. We didn't think twice about going in. We climbed the stairs and stopped at the entrance, looking for a place to deposit our shoes. A teenager approached.

"Welcome, Madame," he proclaimed, beaming from ear to ear, "I will happy to watch your shoe!"

"Thank you very much," I responded and handed over three pairs of shoes to the young watchman. The temple was just as we expected: a quiet retreat from the urban jungle outside. It was almost bare of decorations save the sporadic carvings of various deities. The smell of incense permeated the otherwise stale air of the temple. The marble floor was scalding hot under the blazing April sun. We looked around and found a thin filthy rug in an area partially shaded by the temple roof. We had been in India too long to care about the condition of the floor coverings. We made ourselves comfortable amidst the rug stains, our backs leaning against the temple walls. I took out a bottle of water from my bag and passed it to the kids. Julian took the bottle and carefully examined it. We had not been able to find spring water in India; all the commercially sold water bottles were purified. Every now and then, we came across a familiar brand: Aquafina. More often than not, however, the bottles we bought were of some obscure local making. This one was no exception.

"Dislaren," Julian read aloud, "purified water. Bottled in India. Ingredients: water, extra bacteria added."

The three of us burst out laughing at the joke. It had taken us two weeks to find humor in the dirt and lack of creature comforts. As we drank our bacteria-fortified water in the cool shade of the temple, I observed an exchange between two Western tourists who, like us, had found their way to the temple.

"So, how long have you been in India?" asked the older British girl of the seemingly younger German traveler.

"About three weeks now," responded the German. "And you?"

"It was two years last month. I came for two weeks and never left. I fell in love with India."

I contemplated that conversation for quite awhile. We had been in India long enough to have become sufficiently aware of its unique customs, colorful sights and sounds, dirty hotels, and smelly streets. We had become less sensitive to Indian toilets and stained bed linens. We had stopped holding our noses every time they were assaulted by foul smells. We had learned to enjoy the country for what it was, not for what we would like it to be. Yet, I desperately longed for a long hot shower. And I very much wished to be able to brush my teeth without having to fetch a bottle of water. Could I live in India for two years? I never say never, but it would be difficult for me. I admired the young woman for being able to put up with a lack of luxuries for the experience of a cultural immersion. I wished I could do that. Perhaps when I was younger, I reassured myself.

On leaving the temple, I handed over the ticket to the shoe-watcher at the gate. "Thirty rupees, Madame," announced the wily teenager with a big grin.

"Thirty? But the sign says two rupees per pair. That would be six for three." If I hadn't been so appalled by the audacity, I would have laughed out loud. The boy clearly did not notice a hint of amusement in my face, because he silently handed us the shoes and shrugged.

We spent the rest of the afternoon wandering around the tiny streets of Udaipur. In one of its shops, Fillip found the coveted opal. It was the perfect size and shape for his neck, but there was one problem: it was part of a woman's earring. We convinced the shop owner to take the opal out of the earring and hang it on a silver chain. Within an hour, my son was the proud wearer of an Indian opal necklace. We also stopped in a tiny souvenir shop to pick up a present for my husband, who had opened his own company three years prior. The kids and I decided to bring him a small bronze statuette of a Hindu deity for good luck. We tried to decide between Lakshmi, a goddess of good fortune, and Ganesha, a god who removes obstacles. After long discussions, we decided to buy both. After all, one can't have too much good luck and fortune.

Before dinner, we went to the hotel pool for a quick swim. The pool was located on top of the roof and had magnificent views of the lakes and palaces of Udaipur. As was often the case, we were the only hotel guests enjoying the cool water. The kids did laps while I read in the shade of one of the cabanas set up next to the pool. It was then that I noticed a conspicuous rash on Julian's face. The rash circled his mouth and stretched to the bottom of his left cheek. I dug into my deep makeup case as soon as we walked into our room to find a tube of hydrocortisone cream and slathered it on his face.

"There, just don't touch your face with your dirty fingers anymore," I warned. "I'm not sure how you managed to get that, but whatever you do, please try to wash your hands and not touch your face anymore. We only have two more days to go."

"Yes, Mom," sighed Julian, and we set out for the restaurant.

The restaurant was next to the pool on the other side of the roof and boasted of being the best in town—it said so right on its menu. In addition to the by-then familiar Indian dishes, it offered a number of Western delicacies. It didn't take us long to choose unfamiliar items, as we were happy to taste something new. We were quickly disappointed. As good as the food was, it was typical Indian cuisine, even if it did bear Western names.

We woke up early the next morning. After an afternoon in Udaipur, we would take an overnight train back to New Delhi. We met Sanjay outside of the hotel. This was the day on which, two weeks ago, he consented to join us for lunch. It was our last day with Sanjay, and the kids and I were feeling very sad. Over the last few weeks, Sanjay had become a fourth member of the family. We became so accustomed to his "Good morning, Madame" and "Good night, children" that it was bizarre for us to imagine starting our morning or ending our evening without him. The best parts of our road trips were filled listening to Sanjay's stories about life in his village in Kashmir. Every morning as we climbed into the white Ambassador, we inquired if there was any news from Sanjay's home. He, in turn, would share with us his son's scholastic achievements, harvest reports from the family farm, and his wife's requests for various household goods. We were going to miss not just this jovial kind man, but his whole remote mountain village.

"Today, Madame, I will take you to lakes. Udaipur lakes are the most beautiful lakes. Very pretty and there is much to see and much to do there," announced Sanjay. Then he gave us the name of our first destination, and I could not, for the life of me, figure out what he had said.

"I'm sorry, Sanjay, to where?"

He repeated himself. It didn't help.

"Where, Mom?" my kids called from the backseat. I smiled at Sanjay and turned to them.

"Are you kidding me?" I hissed at the little darlings. "Do you think anyone could understand that?"

"So you have no clue?"

"None," I responded without moving my lips and stretching my face into an even bigger smile for Sanjay.

We got out of the Ambassador in front of an inconspicuous gate. There was no sign at the door and no clue as to what lay behind it. We looked around and after the routine of paying the cashier and showing the ticket to the gentleman positioned right next to the cashier, we walked through the gates. The only English signs we found were those identifying the numerous exotic plants and flowers scattered all around the grounds of whatever it was that we were observing. We concluded that we were probably in some kind of a botanical garden. After walking around its grounds for less than an hour, we decided to head back to the car. There were only so many varieties of flowers prepubescent boys could tolerate in one morning.

Our next destination promised to be more exciting. We were heading down to the lakes. Udaipur is a city of lakes. We were looking forward to spending a leisurely afternoon at the lakes before heading back into the madness of the trains and the chaos of New Delhi. Sanjay dropped us off at a quiet promenade and pointed in the direction of a ticket booth. We set out to choose a vessel on which to see the lakes. Approaching the riverfront, we were immediately surrounded by a number of boatmen, each praising his particular craft and trying to convince us that nothing in this world would make us happier than an afternoon in his company.

"Wow, Mom, they have paddleboats. I always wanted to ride one."

We were still surrounded by the boatmen, so Fillip's outburst almost started a fistfight, as the paddleboat owners, seizing their moment, began elbowing others out of the way.

I put on the well-trained wide grin and turned to my younger son. "Let's see what we want to do," I said slowly through my teeth, speaking solely for the sake of the boatmen. If there was anything I knew for certain, it was that there was no way we were riding the paddleboats that afternoon.

With the same stationary grin on my face, I pulled the kids a few steps from the ticket window and squatted down to their level. "Are you out of your mind?" I hissed. "Have you looked at this water? If you so much as dip a toe in this lake, you will need emergency medical care."

"Oh, Mom, it's not so bad!" argued Julian.

"Not so bad? Have you looked down there? It's not as bad as Varanasi, I give you that. But there is garbage floating near the shore. Now, I agree, the water in the middle of the lake looks somewhat trash-free, but we cannot take a chance; a paddleboat is just out of the question."

We finally settled on the relative safety of a motorboat around the lake. We purchased our ticket and walked down to the dock with a proud boat owner. With his beaming face, he looked like he had just signed a deal with Microsoft, rather than having been chosen for a mere ride in his boat. But this was a slow season, and I had not noticed anyone at the lake with the exception of a few local families enjoying the paddleboats; clearly, they did not have the same concerns.

I questioned my choice as I got on the boat. Though I had not been keeping myself on the strictest diet while in India, I still saw no reason for the boat to shake as violently as it did when I stepped onto it. For a split second, I contemplated grabbing the kids and leaving the boat. It is likely that the boatman read that intention on my face, as he started the engine just as I got my second leg onto the boat. After a rocky start, the ride itself was a lovely change for us. For the first time in India, we could just sit back and enjoy the view; there were no crowds, no peddlers, and no dirt or foul smell to distract us from the beauty of the Udaipur lakes, which were surrounded by palaces. Wind blew through our hair, and engine noise made it impossible to hear each other, so we just enjoyed the moment. We knew that the hustle and bustle of New Delhi awaited us, followed by the everyday grind of work and school. This was our thirty minutes of quiet time.

Sanjay waited for us at the docks as we came up from the water. We were on our way to have lunch at a restaurant he chose. We trusted him implicitly. The restaurant was inside a local inn. We would never have known there was a restaurant inside, as it was located in a Moorish courtyard surrounded by the building walls. Having lunch with Sanjay liberated the kids from utensils. As was the local custom, Sanjay scooped up the various bean dishes with pieces of *roti* he held in his hands. The kids were more than happy to follow suit. Within minutes, neither of my kids was recognizable behind globs of *dal* on their faces. Sanjay's skill came with years of practice. The kids did not stand a chance.

It was our last supper, after which Sanjay's life would remain unchanged. He would continue to drive foreigners around India, collect small amounts of rupees to send home, and live for those few days a year when he got to visit his family. We were just another fare. To us, however, Sanjay brought a world we had only read about in books. It was a world where people worked a lot and got paid little. It was a world where leprosy survived and infants died. It was a world where running water was a luxury and the whole world was your toilet. Sanjay was a part of that world. And in the last two weeks we spent with him, he had brought that world closer to us. He made it real;

he gave it a name. He made us more than just mere spectators—he made us care.

I handed Sanjay an envelope with tip money. I knew that it was enough money for his son to get books for a year, for his wife to get a few new dresses, and for the farm to get more fertilizer. But somehow I felt dirty handing over the money to Sanjay. I was patching a pipe that was about to burst, and all I had was a bandage. I wished I could do more.

Sanjay asked the waiters to pack us some dinner to take with us on the train. It was still Passover so I settled for a few dry *roti* with hard-boiled eggs, while the kids ordered a scrumptious meal of eggs, *naan*, *dal*, and some other delicacies I could not pronounce. I took photos of Sanjay and the kids in front of the Ambassador and promised to send them to Sanjay's boss to forward to Sanjay. A few days after I returned to the U.S., I kept my promise.

We drove to the train station in silence. The station was much smaller and a lot less menacing than its New Delhi counterpart. By that point we felt at home enough to promptly elbow our way through the crowd to find our train. We headed directly to the front of the train to find the first-class car. I reviewed the passenger list to find our names. Sure enough, next to ours was another name, unknown to us. We were going to have another overnight neighbor. I secretly hoped it would be our previous bunkmate. I knew it was a vain hope.

This time around, we didn't bother asking the conductor for new bedding. Yes, the sheets had stains—many stains. We didn't care. We were dirty and smelly and blended right into those sheets. Julian, whose dirty feet had preoccupied him so much on our first overnight train, engaged in a competition with his brother as to whose feet housed more grime. I am not sure which one of them won. I was too afraid to look at my own feet, as I worried that I might just be the winner. After the usual commotion at the station, the train started to move. There were still only three of us in the sleeper. I let myself entertain hope that it would remain that way.

"Excuse me, sir," I called over to the conductor, who ran up and down the car creating a grand illusion of activity and chaos. After the third "excuse me," he finally stuck his head into our sleeper, although his face conveyed a faint annoyance with the fact that I had disrupted his run.

"Yes, Madame, what is it?"

"Is anyone else supposed to be in this sleeper, or are we alone?" I inquired rather cautiously.

"There will be another gentleman at a further station," responded the conducted dryly. "Anything else?"

"No, thank you." We quietly withdrew into the confines of our sleeper and reluctantly opened our dinner bags. Even though I had not eaten meat for more than a decade, the thought of another dry *roti* made me insanely jealous of the sausages packed neatly into the kids' bags. While Julian happily chased down his sausage with a glass of hot *chai*, which he had hurried to order the minute we got on the train, I tried to work up an appetite for the hard-boiled egg. My efforts were in vain. Seeing Fillip cringe at the first bite of his food somewhat justified my own struggle, and we ultimately decided that the sooner we got to bed, the quicker the night would pass.

I headed out to the lavatory. Two train workers were sitting cross-legged on the floor in front of the so-called Western bathroom. On the floor in front of them was some *dal* in metal bowls, which they were dutifully scooping up with brown pieces of *naan*. I felt deeply ashamed of my earlier dinner grievance.

After a brief stint with a toothbrush and a bottle of water, I crawled under the stained sheets and eventually fell asleep. We were awakened about an hour later by a noisy commotion taking place around our compartment. There was a lot of stomping, luggage throwing, and shuffling, all accompanied by a continuous loud phone conversation in Hindi. I opened my eyes to look at the time; it was after midnight. Our compartment mate had arrived. He was a large gentleman with bulging eyes and a balding head. What he lacked in looks, he compensated for in jewels and aplomb. There was hardly a place on his body that was not adorned with a flashy piece of gold jewelry; from a thick chain around his equally thick neck to a ruby pinky ring that looked like it was permanently etched into his stubby finger, this gentlemen clearly wished to ensure that everyone around him understood he was a man of means. He was certainly not a man of class or graciousness.

He didn't care that it was past twelve o'clock and his roommates were trying to sleep. None of that mattered to him as he stomped around the train car, barking orders to the three porters carrying his never-ending stock of luggage. Without missing a beat, he barked something at the conductor, who followed him into our sleeper. The previously menacing conductor whimpered something in return and promptly made his exit. With all of his entourage gone, the stout gentlemen continued to shout something seemingly important into the phone, as the kids and I tried in vain to get some sleep. When he finally fell silent, I lay awake listening to the rhythm of the rail.

How different this ride was from our previous one. It seemed that we had lived through centuries in the last couple of weeks. Had we become wiser? Probably not, but we definitely had grown more tolerant and attuned to the many peculiarities, inconsistencies, and injustices that comprise the vast enigma that is India. I thought about all the things we'd seen and experienced and realized that I would never be able to fully comprehend or relay most of them.

I was still enthralled in a deep philosophical discussion with myself, when the sky outside began to lighten. Soon, the first rays of the morning sun started to illuminate the fields along the tracks. Groups of women emerged from the surrounding villages and spread out in overgrown bushes surrounding the railways, which served as the communal latrine. The women, in their modesty, had to take care of their ablutions before sunrise. The men would appear later, in full sunlight, squatting in bunches along the tracks. Some were chatting with each other and some read newspapers. This was a universe parallel to my own, with its jetted tubs and electric bidets. I felt like a voyeur intruding on people's most private moments. I grabbed a bottle of water and headed out to the train lavatory. Once there, unfortunately, no matter how many times I tried to remind myself of the shame I had felt earlier when complaining about my own deprivation, I still could not bring myself to use the filthy public bathroom, and after a quick wash and brush, I abruptly left.

Chapter 17

NEW DELHI

It was six o'clock in the morning when we pulled up to the train station in New Delhi. We stepped out onto the platform and were quickly swallowed by the live mass of the station. It was just as chaotic and frenzied as when we had left, but we were no longer intimidated. We elbowed our way outside of the station and I promptly dialed Jawahar on my phone.

"Ah, *namaste*, Madame!" screamed Jawahar into the receiver. "The driver is waiting for you at the station."

"We are at the station, Jawahar. Where at the station is he?"

What followed was a complicated set of instructions that sent us back inside to elbow our way to the opposite end of the street. Once on the street, we had to fight our way through a mob of taxi drivers who were firmly blocking the exit, eager to offer their services to each passenger coming out the door. The situation quickly became aggravating, as the longer we walked up and down the block, the more we convinced the drivers of our need for a ride. I dialed Jawahar again. Another set of complicated instructions sent us back inside the station in search of yet another street exit.

Forty minutes and two more exits later, we were comfortably seated in a small Toyota Sedan. "My name is Prim, Madame," announced the young man at the wheel. "I will be your driver for today."

"Very nice to meet you," I said, stifling the urge to scream "finally."

"Where you would like go, Madame?"

"First, Prim, let's find a place to eat. We have not yet had breakfast."

"I'm starving, Mom," Julian added helpfully.

"Would you like Indian breakfast or Western breakfast, Madame?" inquired Prim

"Western!" screamed the children in unison.

"Fine, Madame, I find you restaurant."

That was easier said than done. For the next fifty minutes, we circled all over the new and old districts of New Delhi in search of an open restaurant that served breakfast. At one point, we even contemplated McDonald's. Our painful search led us to a small hotel in Old Delhi. Prim left us at the entrance to the restaurant and went inside to discuss something with the resident waiter. He soon emerged and said in a whisper, "You can eat here, but it is not allowed. You will have to pay waiter."

I had spent the first twelve years of my life in the Soviet Union. Bribes were a way of life; the question was never whom to bribe, but how much and with what. I was too young to partake in the practice, but my parents had to navigate the complicated bribery maze every day. Because it was such a mundane, daily affair, children like me were, if not well versed, at least closely familiar with the routine.

"No problem, Prim," I quickly consented. "Just let me know how much."

As my starving children were helping themselves to a buffet of croissants and cold cereals, I quietly slipped a few rupees to Prim, who passed them into the waiter's hand as the two smoked a cigarette outside. On a fed stomach, things looked a lot brighter.

Full and happy, we could discuss our last day's itinerary. The first stop on our route was going to be Humayun's tomb. It was the only attraction in Delhi that we wished to return to and photograph. Walking through the tomb, we were definitely more confident in our step, more bold with the gawking teenagers, and less friendly with frivolous men. As we proceeded to photograph the tomb complex, I couldn't shake the feeling of being watched. As any sane person would, I dismissed it as temporary insanity. Then Fillip looked up and said, "Mom, have you noticed that hawk has been following us since we got here?"

I had noticed a large hawk as soon as we arrived at the complex. The ominous bird hovered above us continuously, at times dangerously close to our heads. After the initial alarm, I was calmed and even comforted by that bird. It seemed to be looking out for us, ready to strike at anyone meaning us harm. I almost laughed out loud at my own absurdity.

"I did notice," I responded. "It's OK, it's just a bird."

"Where do you wish to go now, Madame?" asked Prim as we got into the car.

I took out a piece of paper and read an address that meant nothing to me.

"Do you know where it is, Prim?" I asked

"Yes, Madame, I know street. I will find it."

We drove into the streets of New Delhi and Prim pulled up in front of the gate of an ordinary house.

"Are you sure this is the address, Prim?"

"Yes, Madame, it is," Prim reassured us. "Should I wait here?"

"Yes, please," I responded as we stepped out of the car.

The kids and I walked through an iron gate that could have belonged to any suburban home, from California to New Castle to New Delhi. It was only when we were inside the courtyard that we saw a large Star of David prominently displayed on the front of the building. We had arrived at the only synagogue in New Delhi. A middle-aged Indian woman met us in front of the gate.

"Can I help you?" she asked us in a tone that was more bored than suspicious.

"Can we please see the rabbi?" I asked.

"The rabbi is resting," responded the housekeeper, expecting us to go away.

I looked at my watch. It was twelve-thirty in the afternoon.

"Can you ask him to see us?" I insisted.

"He may be sleeping," protested the housekeeper.

"Please wake him up," I persisted, and the woman disappeared inside the building.

What emerged five minutes later was an unhappy man in his undershirt and pajama pants, clearly aroused from his siesta against his wishes. "May I help you?" He looked us up and down, trying to gauge what emergency had disturbed his well-deserved afternoon rest.

I introduced myself and the children. I explained that we were from New York and wanted to visit the local synagogue and chat with the rabbi before going back home. Julian was studying for his bar mitzvah. He had a coin given to him by a New York rabbi who had asked him to donate it in New Delhi.

Reluctantly, the rabbi opened the doors and we found ourselves inside the synagogue. It was not lavishly decorated. As a matter of fact, as far as synagogues go, while still in the Asian style, it was a lot less flashy than most of its sisters in the East. The kids donned *kippahs* and we sat down to chat with the rabbi. We told him about Julian's upcoming bar mitzvah, about life in New York, and about my travails in India during Passover. He told us how sad he was that his whole congregation was comprised of only about forty people, and that included the non-Jewish spouses of Jews who, for one reason or another, had found themselves on work assignments in India. He boasted about how, on the first day of Passover, he had had *matzah* imported from Israel. I sighed, thinking about all the *poppadom* I had ingested in lieu of the traditional unleavened bread.

Within fifteen minutes, we were family. He told us about his children back in Israel. We told him about our loved ones in New York. We related to each other as lost souls who had found themselves at the end of the Earth and had to catch up on all the time they had lost apart from each other. There was nothing in particular that we wanted other than to meet someone who was like us—a wandering Jew who, if only for five minutes, wanted to fit in.

When it was time to leave, the rabbi offered to pronounce a traditional blessing. We quickly agreed, and as we bowed our heads, the rabbi touched each of us, mumbling words that rabbis have been mumbling for years, wishing us a safe journey and a happy life. At the end, he was just as reluctant to let us leave as he had been, at first, to let us in. He insisted that we photograph ourselves in front of every

Star of David and every memorial plaque the synagogue displayed, even offering to take a group photo of us. After leaving him with my New York phone number, we finally walked out of the gate.

"Ready to go, now?" asked Prim as we got back into the Toyota.

"Yes, Prim. Let's go have lunch."

"Can I ask you a question, Madame?" Prim said as we pulled away from the curb.

"Sure, Prim, what is it?"

"What was that place you just went?"

"It was a synagogue," I said.

"What is a synagogue?" I was quickly brought back to Earth. I was still in India, that parallel universe where things that were ordinary to us were not necessarily so ordinary.

"It's a temple for the Jews," I offered.

"Jews?"

"Jewish People."

Prim seemed just as confused but did not ask any more questions. I let the subject go.

We had some free time after lunch. "How about the zoo?" I offered. "I read that the zoo has rare Bengal tigers." My offer was accepted, and, before long, we found ourselves in front of a large entrance to the park. To our dismay, there was no kiosk with water. In the hopes of finding one inside the zoo, we paid the admission fee and passed through the gates.

We quickly realized that obtaining bottled water would be a challenge. The only water the zoo offered was flowing out of drinking fountains. There was, however, a soda vendor, so we settled for a bottle of orange-flavored soda. Less than ten minutes later, we found out why the kiosks were so abundant throughout the zoo; in the sweltering heat of a midday Indian sun, the sweet drink turned into sweat in less than a minute, leaving us just as thirsty almost immediately after ingesting it. We must've bought a dozen sodas, chugging them down as soon as they were paid for.

Before we saw any animals, we stopped in front of a sign reading, "Beware of stray monkeys." Considering the hordes of monkeys we had seen everywhere from New Delhi to Jaipur, the sign seemed unnecessary. Nonetheless, after walking for about twenty minutes and seeing no animals, we seriously longed for an encounter with a monkey. It was a zoo, after all.

"Mom, I need to find a bathroom!" Fillip suddenly declared in a tone that sent me searching for the nearest bathroom immediately. Unfortunately, the nearest bathroom was still too far, as the poor child suddenly had been stricken by a severe upset stomach. The next five minutes were the longest in our lives. We ran, frantically looking for a bathroom, which seemed as elusive as the zoo's animals. By the time a bathroom was in sight, Fillip was racing. For a moment, I doubted he would make it. I was playing out the worst-case scenarios in my head while observing a wild monkey stealing food from a cage with a sign that said "goats" on it. Julian, who had accompanied his brother, soon emerged from the bathroom to announce that all was well. Fillip came out a few minutes later with a sour grimace on his face and proceeded to tell a long tale of a hornet circling around his stall and a bathroom attendant who wanted money; I never did figure out whether the attendant wanted money for chasing away the hornet or for the virtue of simply being there. All I knew was that we had just averted a major disaster.

The rest of our day was spent rather uneventfully. We walked through a small fort that was surrounded by a park. It would've been lovely at any other time, but by then, we were ready to go home. As much as we had enjoyed our time in India, we were looking forward to hot showers, clean toilets, and sheets without stains. We missed brushing our teeth with running water and having bagels for breakfast. We missed home.

Walking through the automatic airport doors, we felt one step closer to home. Staring us in the face was a true symbol of America: a Subway restaurant. Passover had just ended, so we made a beeline straight for the counter. We only had a few rupees left. Not wanting to change any more currency we could not use, we carefully chose the menu to fit our meager budget. The clerk calculated the total, and I couldn't help but to assume a wide grin: it was the exact amount of rupees I had in my wallet. But this was India; nothing would ever be simple. As we were about to leave the counter, the clerk said, "Sorry, Madame, I forgot to count second water."

"We will take just one water," I said, proud of my Solomon-like wisdom. We devoured our sandwiches right there on a metal bench next to the Subway counter. Any five-star restaurant in New York or Paris paled in comparison to the taste of those sandwiches. We savored every bite and licked every crumb off the parchment paper in which the sandwiches were rolled. No dinner we had ever had before or after would compare to that one, the one we finished in five minutes on the bench of the New Delhi Airport.

Full and happy, I headed for the ladies room. I walked into a typical airport bathroom: metal stalls, plain white tile. And then I heard, "Mommy, it is so beautiful here!" A little girl of eight or nine couldn't control her excitement at the sight of an airport bathroom. How different my world was from that little girl's.

The boys, in the meantime, came out of the men's room in a total panic. Apparently, even at the airport, their long hair aroused suspicion. One of the men in the washroom had insisted they leave immediately because it was for men only. It wasn't until Julian pulled down his shorts to prove that he and Fillip did indeed belong there that the man quieted down.

Then we arrived at airport security. It was separated into two sections: men's and women's. One of the airport staff tried sending my sons to the women's line. "Should I pull down my pants again, Mom?" asked Julian in total frustration.

"No, please don't," I shouted, totally terrified that he just might. I took his passport and waved it in front of the security men, saying, "Boy, see? Boy!" I kept repeating it until both of my children made it safely to the other side of the line.

Our fourteen-hour flight back was spent dreaming about soap and hot water. As soon as I had sat down in my seat, I felt my filth. In between our frequent trips to the bathroom to appease our terribly upset stomachs, we scratched and itched and argued about who would take the first shower. I finally forfeited my rights, as the kids had school that day. I found myself fantasizing about standing in a hot shower, covering my body with soap, and feeling the bubbles on my skin. Something that seemed so routine only three weeks ago had turned into a luxury that I just couldn't wait to sample.

"Do you notice anything?" asked Fillip as we stepped off the plane into an empty terminal. It was not yet five o'clock in the morning. The terminal was abandoned with the exception of a few sleepy travelers awaiting their connection.

"I notice nothing, what is it?" I had just returned from a journey of fourteen hours and hundreds of years. Thinking was not something I could call do on demand at the moment.

"How do you not notice?" Fillip was visibly excited. "No one is staring at us!" I felt for him. He really had been disturbed by the attention he had received back in India. It was over now, and the kids couldn't wait to see their father, who was picking us up outside of the terminal.

It was a cold April morning. The sun was just beginning to come up and the chill in the air was unusual for that time of year. We pulled away from the airport.

"I'm sorry," said my husband, "can I open the windows? I can't breathe."

"You can't breathe? Are you all right?" I became alarmed; what could have happened in the short time we had been gone?

"I'm all right," he reassured me. "But the three of you smell so bad you are making me nauseous." The kids and I burst out laughing.

"So," said my husband as he opened every car window and stuck his head far enough out of the car to not smell us, "tell me all about your trip."

"Where would I begin?" I mused.

Indeed, where would I begin?